Working with God Through Intercessory PRAYER

Working with God Through Intercessory PRAYER

D. Edmond Hiebert

BOB JONES UNIVERSITY PRESS
Greenville, South Carolina 29614

Library of Congress Cataloging-in-Publication Data

Hiebert, D. Edmond (David Edmond), 1910-
    Working with God through intercessory prayer / by D. Edmond Hiebert.

    Includes bibliographical references and indexes.
    ISBN 0-89084-598-0
    1. Intercessory prayer—Christianity.   2. Bible—Prayers.
  I. Title.
  BV210.2.H53   1991
  248.3'2—dc20   91-28460
                                                                 CIP

Working with God Through Intercessory Prayer
by D. Edmond Hiebert

This book is a revised edition of *Working with God: Scriptural Studies in Intercession* (1987), published by Carlton Press.

All Scripture quotations, unless otherwise noted, are from the King James Version of the Bible. Quotation from other translations does not necessarily indicate an endorsement by the publisher of all of the contents of such translations.

A careful effort has been made to trace the ownership of poems included in this book in order to secure permission to reprint copyright material and to make full acknowledgement of their use. If any error or omission has occurred, it is purely inadvertent and will be corrected in subsequent editions, provided written notification is made to the publisher.

NOTE:
The fact that materials produced by other publishers are referred to in this volume does not constitute an endorsement by Bob Jones University Press of the content or theological position of materials produced by such publishers. The position of Bob Jones University Press, and the University itself, is well known. Any references and ancillary materials are listed as an aid to the reader and in an attempt to maintain the accepted academic standards of the publishing industry.

ISBN 0-89084-598-0

Printed in the United States of America

20   19   18   17   16   15   14   13   12   11   10 9 8 7 6

Contents

Abbreviations

For the full publishing information on these versions, see the Bibliography.

ASV   American Standard Version (1901)

KJV   King James Version (1611)

NASB   *New American Standard Bible* (1971)

NEB   *New English Bible* (2nd ed. 1979)

NIV   New International Version (1978)

Preface

Prayer is indeed "the Christian's vital breath." It is also God's gracious arrangement whereby His saints are privileged to work together with Him in furthering His sovereign purpose. In intercession God brings His saints into cooperation with Him in accomplishing His work in the world. "Prayer unites puny man to Almighty God in miraculous partnership. It is the most noble and most essential ministry God gives to His children–but is the most neglected."[1] This is the basic message of this volume.

The opening chapter presents the nature and privilege of working with God through intercessory prayer; the second chapter delineates this ministry through a brief consideration of a number of New Testament passages dealing with the work of intercession. The next two chapters give a fuller exposition of two of the passages touched on in Chapter 2. Chapters 5 through 7 are studies of three Biblical passages concerning men who had learned to work with God through prayer. Chapters 8 and 9 concentrate on the seriousness of our failure to apprehend and practice adequately the ministry of intercession and the divine response to that failure. The concluding chapter is an appeal to take up this ministry through a consideration of the Biblical story of Daniel working with God through prayer.

This theme of working by prayer was first made precious to the writer's heart some thirty years ago after a protracted illness. Over the years the essence of several of these messages has appeared in varied Christian periodicals.

Notes

[1] P. J. Johnson, *Operation World. A Handbook for World Intercession* (Bromley, Kent, England: STL Publications, 1978), p. 15.

I

Working by Prayer

Believers have the high privilege of working with God through intercessory prayer. This privilege is grounded in the divinely ordained nature of prayer.

I. *The Privilege of Prayer*

> *The effectual fervent prayer of a righteous man availeth much.*
> (James 5:16)

Prayer is a powerful and effective means of working with God. This concept of prayer will appear questionable and presumptuous only to the individual who maintains that prayer effects merely a subjective change in the one praying and produces no objective changes in life. But the believer who in simple faith accepts the teaching of Scripture concerning the nature and impact of intercession finds such a view credible and challenging.

James categorically asserts, "The effectual fervent prayer of a righteous man availeth much" (5:16) and in confirmation cites the results of the prayers of the prophet Elijah (5:17-18). His prayers produced objective changes in the affairs of the nation of Israel. The word here rendered "prayer" was restricted in common usage to petitionary prayer; one may well render it "supplication." The term centers attention on something desired by the one who utters the petition. His petition probably had the ultimate aim of furthering the true spiritual interests of the nation of Israel. His prayers certainly produced shattering objective changes in the life of the idolatrous nation. Although his work did not produce the spiritual revival that Elijah had hoped for in the nation, it provided an undeniable display of the reality of working by prayer.

James declares that the prayer of "a righteous man" produces great results. His statement leaves the contents of the supplication unrestricted; the only limitation is that the petitioner must be "a righteous" individual. James assumes that the individual has been declared righteous by faith in Christ, but his designation further implies that he is righteous in character and conduct. He who would work with God through prayer cannot harbor unrighteousness in his life nor can his petition be designed to promote any unrighteousness. Such a person is assured that his prayer "availeth much," is strong or able to do much. It possesses a strength which enables it to overcome opposition and achieve amazing victories.

The words "effectual fervent" as a description of such praying are the rendering in the King James Version of a single word, a present-tense participle which stands emphatically at the end of the sentence. The term denotes a power working inwardly; our English word "energy" is derived from the noun form of this verb. Such praying is an energetic, activating power. It explains why the prayer of a righteous person is so strong. The participle may be either in the middle or the passive voice. If passive, the meaning is that such prayer is so powerful because it is being empowered from above (cf. Rom. 8:26). If in the middle voice, the meaning is that the prayer of a righteous individual keeps on putting forth its energy to get the petition answered. Under either view the term enforces the power of godly praying.

The words of James establish that the prophet's prayers made a tremendous impression on succeeding generations. His power over nature does not imply that by prayer he could suspend the laws of nature at will. Rather, Elijah confidently made his audacious petitions to Jehovah because he was conscious that they were in harmony with the will of God. He could confidently persist in his request for rain (I Kings 18:42-44) because he knew that God had promised to send the rain he was asking for (I Kings 18:1). He could persevere in prayer because he knew his petition was in harmony with the expressed purpose of God.

The Old Testament makes no reference to the praying of Elijah in connection with his bold announcement to Ahab that there would be no further rain or dew without his word (I Kings

17:1). But the statement of James, "and he prayed again" (5:18), implies that the two prayers he cites were of the same character and quality. It seems obvious that Elijah would not have made his open declaration to Ahab, with its disastrous national consequences, without a prior revelation to him of the divine procedure in dealing with the idolatrous nation. His prayers, with their far-reaching impact, demonstrate that "the prophet's communion with God was so intimate that the Spirit could reveal to him not only the purpose of the Lord in these respects, but also the very time when they would come to pass."[1] Knowing the will of God is the sure foundation for effective prayer. "And this is the confidence that we have in him, that, if we ask any thing according to his will, he heareth us" (I John 5:14).

The Scripture reveals that even the fulfillment of an explicit prophecy is somehow dependent upon the prayers of the recipients. In Ezekiel 36 we have a marvelous prophecy of God's dealings with the nation of Israel in the future. The Lord declares how He will cleanse the Israelites, give them a new heart, and cause them to walk in His statutes. Then in verse 37 we read the striking words, "Thus saith the Lord God; I will yet for this be enquired of by the house of Israel, to do it for them." The promise, already delineated, will be fulfilled in response to the prayers of Israel for it.

When we apprehend the Scriptural teaching that prayer is a definite means of working with God, we realize that this teaching is fully in keeping with His gracious character. God yearns to take His children into His confidence and let them share with Him in the accomplishment of His purposes. He has so arranged this world that there is a definite place for answered prayer in the divine government. He deliberately so constituted things so that His believing children may have, and are invited to have, a definite share in the fulfillment of His saving purpose for mankind through intercessory prayer. The Scriptures are replete with illustrations of how the cause of the Lord was furthered as God answered the prayers of His people.

> There is a power that man can wield,
>   When mortal aid is vain,
> That eye, that arm, that love to reach,
>   That list'ning ear to gain.

That power is prayer, which soars on high
   Through Jesus to the throne,
And moves the hand which moves the world
   To bring salvation down.

The glorious possibility of working by prayer, revealed in the Scriptures, is confirmed in the experience of multitudes of God's people. James was desirous that his readers would enter into a personal experience thereof. He cited the experiences of Elijah, not as unique and unrepeatable instances, but as encouragement for them likewise to avail themselves of this divinely established privilege. He reminded them that Elijah "was a man subject to like passions as we are" (James 5:17). He had the same nature and was subject to the feelings and experiences of other men. If God answered his prayers, He would also answer theirs.

II. *The Nature of Prayer*

And I say unto you, Ask, and it shall be given you; seek, and ye shall find; knock, and it shall be opened unto you. For every one that asketh receiveth; and he that seeketh findeth; and to him that knocketh it shall be opened. If a son shall ask bread of any of you that is a father, will he give him a stone? or if he ask a fish, will he for a fish give him a serpent? Or if he shall ask an egg, will he offer him a scorpion? If ye then, being evil, know how to give good gifts unto your children: how much more shall your heavenly Father give the Holy Spirit to them that ask him? (Luke 11:9-13)

The privilege of working by prayer is fully in accord with the nature of true prayer. Prayer does not merely consist in our speaking to God. It is not a monologue but rather a dialogue. It is a two-sided affair with God on one side and the believer on the other. The instructive words of our Lord given in Luke 11:9-13 can help us see the proper relation between the two sides.

God's side. The first move in true prayer comes from God's side. He set in operation the practice of prayer by arranging for it and giving us the invitation to pray. Thus we hear our Lord saying, "Ask . . . seek . . . knock." When once we apprehend that the initiative lies with God, we recognize that prayer is not forcing ourselves into the presence of God but rather accepting His gracious invitation. Without His welcome it would be futile for man to attempt to "crash the gates of heaven." Prayer is making use of the grand provision God has made for us.

Such an understanding of the prayers of men makes it clear that an objective answer to prayer is not breaking the laws of the universe, as is sometimes erroneously asserted. The God who established the laws of the universe arranged for the practice of prayer with its answers. Prayer, then, is itself one of the laws of the universe. God may at times supersede a lower law by a higher law in response to the cry of His saints, but that is in accord with the divine arrangement.

Having arranged for prayer, God now invites, yea, urges us to make use of the provision. The ringing words of Christ, "Ask . . . seek . . . knock . . . ," are in the imperative mode and constitute a command. It is our duty to enter into this divine provision for intercession. All three imperatives are in the present tense and underline prayer as our continuing duty and privilege.

God further takes the initiative in prayer by creating an urge for prayer in the heart of the believer. The indwelling Holy Spirit turns the heart of the believer Godward (Gal. 4:6) and motivates and aids his prayers (Rom. 8:26-27), while the ascended Lord Jesus Christ Himself makes intercession for the believer before the heavenly throne (Rom. 8:34). The words of Jesus assure us that the Heavenly Father is ever eager to listen to the prayers of His people. How amazing the divine provision of prayer!

Our side. The next move in prayer is on our side. The wondrous provision for prayer having been unveiled, it is up to us to respond to the provision. We must make use of the glorious provision offered to us.

Yet the words of our Lord remind us that working by prayer is a demanding and strenuous activity. It requires determined effort and perseverance. How quickly we give up in our praying; yet our Lord's very words of invitation also urge us to persevere. The force of the present imperatives may well be rendered "Keep on asking . . . keep on seeking . . . keep on knocking." The form of His invitation warns us to expect a delay at times and not to become discouraged but instead to persist until the answer comes. Delays often test the intensity of our desire for the answer and reveal whether or not we really want the request that we are praying for.

God's side. The final move in true prayer is again on God's side: He moves in response to our prayer. Prayer is not just a subjective exercise, valuable for the influence that it has upon us personally; it brings a response from God. That is the emphasis Jesus makes in the passage before us. Having initiated the prayer privilege, God will not ignore or mock our prayers. He joins each summons to prayer with His promise of an answer: "it shall be given . . . ye shall find . . . it shall be opened." "All three promises are categorical, without any 'if' or 'but.' God always hears believing prayer."[2] The answer may not come in the form or manner in which we had requested it, but as a loving Heavenly Father, He will not fail to give the one praying that which is best for him.

Jesus further stresses that God will not fool the supplicant. He enforces this truth by means of three illustrations from daily life. Using the father-son relationship, Jesus insists that a human father will not trick his son. When the son asks the father for bread, the father will not give him a stone, will he? If the son asks for a fish, the father will not give him a serpent, will he? And if the son should ask for an egg, the father will not give him a scorpion, will he? To do so would be entirely contrary to the nature of a human father. Arguing from the lesser to the greater, Jesus then shows that our Heavenly Father will not fool us when we come to Him with our requests at His invitation.

Watchman Nee remarks that whenever God wants to do a spiritual work, He first prompts a man to pray for that which he desires to do because "He desires man to cooperate with Him through prayer."[3] Nee sees all spiritual work as consisting of four steps:

> The first step is that God conceives a thought, which is His will: The second step is that God reveals this will to His children through the Holy Spirit, causing them to know that He has a will, a plan, a demand and expectation: The third step is that God's children return His will by praying to Him, for prayer is responding to God's will–if our heart is wholly one with His heart, we will naturally voice in our prayer what He intends to do: And the fourth step is that God will accomplish this very thing.[4]

Nee cites Ezekiel 36:37 as well as Isaiah 62:6-7 as Scriptural ground for insisting that God works as His people continue to pray for that which it is His will to do.[5] He continues,

> Prayer must originate from God and be responded to by us. Such alone is meaningful prayer, since God's *work* is controlled by

such prayer. How many things the Lord indeed desires to do, yet He does not perform them because His people do not pray.[6]

Working by prayer is the God-ordained privilege of the believer. God graciously invites His children to enter freely into this full-orbed experience of prayer. It is a privilege open to all by faith.

Prayer

Prayer is the mightiest force that men can wield,
A power to which Omnipotence doth yield,
A privilege unparalleled, a way
Whereby our loving Father can display
His interest in His children's need and care.

Jehovah's storehouse is unlocked by prayer,
And faith doth turn the key. Oh! would that men
Did fully prove this wondrous means, for then
Would mightier blessings on the Church be showered,
Her witness owned, her ministers empowered,
And souls ingathered. Then the Gospel's sound
Would soon be heard to earth's remotest bound.

All things are possible if men but pray;
And if God did but limit to a day,
The time in which He'd note the upward glance,
Or fix the place, or name the circumstance,
When, where, or why petition could be brought,
Methinks His presence would by all be sought.

But since He heareth prayer at any time,
For anything, in any place, or clime,
Men lightly value heaven's choicest gift,
And all too seldom do their souls uplift
In earnest pleading at the Throne of Grace.

Oh let us then more often seek His face,
With grateful hearts, remembering while there
To thank our Father that He heareth prayer.

–Author Unknown

Notes

[1]Herbert F. Stevenson, *James Speaks For Today* (Westwood, N.J.: Revell, 1966), p. 117.

[2]R.C.H. Lenski, *The Interpretation of St. Mark's and St. Luke's Gospels* (Columbus, Ohio: Lutheran Book Concern, 1934), p. 871.

[3]Watchman Nee, *Let us Pray* (New York: Christian Fellowship Publishers, 1977), p. 24.

[4]Ibid., p. 24.

[5]Ibid., pp. 25-27.

[6]Ibid., p. 25.

II

The Power of Prayer

But we will give ourselves continually to prayer, and to the ministry of the word. (Acts 6:4)

Prayer is the most powerful and effective means of service in the kingdom of God. God has given a primary place to prayer in the furthering of the gospel. ''Prayer is not begging God to do something which He is loath to do. It is not overcoming reluctance in God. It is enforcing Christ's victory over Satan. It is implementing upon earth Heaven's decisions concerning the affairs of men.''[1] It is the most dynamic work which God has entrusted to His saints, but it is also the most neglected ministry open to the believer.

The Bible clearly reveals that believing prayer is essential for the advancement of the cause of Christ. It is the essential element for Christian victory. Without it, all other means are powerless and ineffectual. Without prayer, toil we ever so hard, our labors for God are vain. The Devil cares but little how many activities we engage in or how many organizations the churches develop, so long as he can keep believers from intensive prayer. Without prayer all the machinery is useless for lack of power.

The twelve apostles were convinced of the primacy of prayer in their work as leaders of the young church in Jerusalem. The surging growth of the church had increased their duties to the point where a division of labor was imperative. Realizing the necessity of conserving their time for the most essential things, they suggested that the matter of ministering to the material needs of the members be delegated to a special group so that they could be free to attend to their primary task, that of continual prayer and the ministry of the Word. And the order of their words indicates that they considered prayer as the more important of the two. They believed that prayer must come even before preaching.

We may marvel at the spiritual power and glorious victories of the early apostolic Church, but we often forget that its constant prayer life was the secret of its strength. Pentecost was preceded by a season of united prayer (Acts 1:14; 2:1). The lame man at the Beautiful Gate was healed by Peter and John as they were going into the temple to pray (3:1). Following their first experience with active persecution, the apostolic group was again filled with the Spirit after a service of united prayer, enabling them to continue preaching the Word of God with boldness (4:31). The seven deacons were chosen that the apostles might be released for the primary work of prayer and preaching (6:1-4). Almost every chapter in the book of Acts contains a reference to or a record of some prayer uttered.

If the Church today would regain the degree of spiritual power of the early Church, it must recover the truth and practice of prayer as a vital working force. The secret of the Church's spiritual power today lies not in the multiplication of organizations, the development of skillfully devised plans of operation, the achievement of organizational unity through the consummation of church mergers, nor yet in the swelling of church rolls, but in persevering, Spirit-taught intercession.

The ministry of intercession is a dynamic service open to every member of the Body of Christ. It is not restricted to those in places of leadership or to those actively engaged in the preaching and teaching of the Word. In Acts 12 "the church," its members as a group, engaged in the dynamic ministry of praying for imprisoned Peter. Neither age nor physical handicap need be a barrier for active service in this ministry.

But before a believer will faithfully engage in this potent ministry, he must have a deep conviction of the place and importance of prayer in the program of God. Such a conviction must be grounded in the Biblical teaching that prayer is a definite means of working for God.

I. *Through Prayer Workers Are Raised up and Sent Forth.*

*The harvest truly is plenteous, but the labourers are few; pray
ye therefore the Lord of the harvest, that he will send forth
labourers into his harvest.* (Matt. 9:37-38)

These memorable words were uttered by our Lord while on
a tour through Galilee with His twelve disciples. The sight of the
needy multitudes on every hand deeply stirred His compassionate
heart. In order also to stir the disciples, He called to their attention
three important facts: the greatness of the harvest, the scarcity of
the laborers, and the duty to pray for laborers. He urged them to
"pray . . . the Lord of the harvest" to send forth the needed
workers. God Himself must raise up and thrust forth the needed
workers. But He works as His people pray. The labor supply for
the harvest of the Lord depends upon the prayers of the saints.

Sometime later, before sending out the seventy in Judea, Jesus
again uttered this plea to pray for workers (Luke 10:2). Before
the seventy were ready to go out as His messengers, they too
needed to be trained in the school of prayer. When God's people
aggressively pray for workers, God will answer that prayer, and
often He calls the very ones that are praying for workers to be
sent forth.

The worldwide evangelistic tour of Dr. R. A. Torrey was born
in an all-night prayer meeting in Chicago. Every Saturday night,
following a public meeting at the Bible Institute, Dr. Torrey with
a few close associates retired to his study to pray for worldwide
revival. Often they prayed until the next morning, going directly
with hearts warm with the sense of God's blessings from the
prayer room to the place of preaching.

One night as this small group was praying, Dr. Torrey felt led
to spontaneously utter the prayer that the Lord send him around the
world on evangelistic missions; that petition continued to be the
burden of their prayers until morning. Shortly afterward two men,
a deputation from Australia, waited upon Dr. Torrey and invited
him to come there for evangelistic missions.[2] Out of that came the
Torrey-Alexander worldwide revival tour in which it is estimated
that one hundred thousand souls professed faith in Christ.

II. *Through Prayer Doors of Opportunity Are Opened for Preaching of the Gospel.*

> *Withal praying also for us, that God would open unto us a door of utterance, to speak the mystery of Christ, for which I am also in bonds: that I may make it manifest, as I ought to speak.* (Col. 4:3-4)

The evangelistic heart of Paul prompted him to request the Colossian Christians to pray for him that a door of opportunity to preach the gospel might be opened to him. Paul was humble enough to ask the very people for whom he was earnestly interceding (Col. 1:9; 2:1) to be praying for him. He was fully convinced that such intercession was effective in the furtherance of the gospel.

As a prisoner Paul felt himself hampered and restricted in his work for the Lord. He craved opportunities to preach the gospel freely and urged believers to pray that such doors might be opened. But for some time the prison doors which confined him did not open. It may well have seemed to those praying for him that their prayers went unanswered. Yet God answered those prayers in a higher way than Paul or the praying Christians realized. Out of those years of imprisonment came those marvelous "Prison Epistles"–Colossians, Ephesians, Philippians, and Philemon– through which the apostle found a door of utterance that has continued down to our own day.

We must pray that the Lord will open the door, but *He* must open it. And He opens the door according to His infinite wisdom.

Through prayer the Lord may open the door to an individual soul. Roland Q. Leavell, a pastor in one of our southern cities, related that one day he found himself in his study with some free time on his hands. He bowed his head and prayed, "Lord, help me to think of someone to win to Christ today." Instantly there flashed into his mind the name of a young man working in one of the stores of the city. He phoned the young man and asked if he were busy, and if not, he would like to talk to him. The youth, who had been spiritually burdened about his salvation, guessed what the pastor wanted to talk to him about; he ran four blocks to the minister's study and there was led to Christ.

Through prayer God can open a large field to the gospel. When in 1887 Jonathan and Rosalind Goforth went to China as missionaries, they were appointed to open a new field in the northern sections of the Province of Honan. Upon learning of their assignment, J. Hudson Taylor of the China Inland Mission wrote them that it was the most antiforeign province in China and advised them, "You must go forward on your knees." For six years they tried to establish a mission in Changte, but every effort was met with utmost hostility. The city was a constant challenge to them and was the object of much prayer. Finally the presbytery which had been formed to direct the work in that area decided to take Changte by faith, and Goforth was asked to open a mission there.

The very next morning Jonathan Goforth was on his way to Changte to secure the needed property for a mission site. All the way to the city he prayed fervently that God would open the hearts of the people and give him the property most suitable for the work. His faith mounted, and he arrived with the assurance that God had heard his prayer. When he made known his purpose, he received not one offer but thirty-five offers, and within three days he was able to secure the very piece of land he had earlier chosen as most ideal for the mission. Mrs. Goforth later testified, "Thus the Lord did break in pieces the gates of brass which had kept us so long from our promised land."[3]

III. *Through Prayer Workers Are Enabled To Speak with Boldness.*

> *Praying always . . . for all saints; and for me, that utterance may be given unto me, that I may open my mouth boldly, to make known the mystery of the gospel.* (Eph. 6:18-19)

As he faces the forces of entrenched evil and satanic wickedness, every Christian worker becomes keenly aware of his need for God-given boldness to preach God's message fearlessly. He realizes that this boldness must come from God and keenly feels his need of the prayers of God's people toward that end.

In his letter to the Ephesians, written while imprisoned in Rome, the Apostle Paul entreated his readers to pray that he may be given the needed boldness to make known the gospel of Christ. If Paul felt his need for the prayers of the obscure Christian friends to whom he was writing, how much more the Christian worker today should feel himself dependent upon the prayers of God's people for the needed boldness to preach in this critical hour.

Christian experience abundantly verifies that God imparts boldness to His messengers in response to the prayers of believers. One of the clearest illustrations of this truth is found in the fourth chapter of Acts. The Sadducees were exasperated because Peter and John, after healing the lame man at the Beautiful Gate, preached the resurrection from the dead through Jesus. After putting the two apostles in jail overnight, the following morning the Sanhedrin strictly forbade them to preach any longer in the name of Jesus. Upon being dismissed, the apostles went to their own company and reported the command of the Sanhedrin. Immediately the whole group gave itself to united prayer, asking God to grant His servants boldness to speak the Word of God. When they had prayed, the place was shaken and they were all filled with the Holy Spirit. Then we read, "And they spake the word of God with boldness. . . . And with great power gave the apostles witness of the resurrection of the Lord Jesus" (Acts 4:31, 33). God still answers such a prayer for boldness to communicate His message because it is according to His will.

IV. *Through Prayer Conditions Favorable for Receiving the Word Are Brought About.*

> *I exhort therefore, that, first of all, supplications, prayers, intercessions, and giving of thanks, be made for all men; for kings, and for all that are in authority; that we may lead a quiet and peaceable life in all godliness and honesty.* (I Tim. 2:1-2)

In I Timothy 2, Paul gives his young assistant some very pointed instructions concerning the place of prayer in the work of the Church. He describes the nature and result of the kind of praying the Church is to engage in. Paul employs four terms to indicate the variety of the prayers to be offered. He indicates that the scope of such praying is to be worldwide. But men live in national groups; hence they are to pray for national rulers. Then he states the result of such prayer: "that we may lead a tranquil and quiet life in all godliness and gravity" (ASV). These words give not the contents of the prayers but the contemplated results of such prayers. As God's people pray for national leaders, conditions favorable to the spread of the gospel are brought about. We need but look at the various nations today to see that the kind of government men live under largely determines whether conditions favorable to the spread of the gospel will prevail. The ultimate purpose of such praying for national leaders is the salvation of souls, as verses three and four indicate. Logic and self-interest thus indicate that whenever believers are alive to their duty of proclaiming the gospel to the masses of their country, they should aggressively pray for their government.

The Old Testament records a number of instances of how the history of Israel was shaped through prayer. We recall, for instance, the mighty prayers of Elijah in his battle against the Baal-worship promoted by Ahab and Jezebel (I Kings 17-18); the prayer of king Hezekiah and the destruction of the army of Sennacherib (II Kings 19; Isa. 37); or the prayer of Nehemiah as the king's cupbearer and his appointment as the governor of Jerusalem (Neh. 1-2).

Through intercessory prayer conditions unfavorable to the gospel in a local community may be changed. Isobel Kuhn in one of her books[4] gives a striking experience in illustration. She relates that during their itinerant work in west China, the missionaries came to a place called Three Clans, where a Christian church was located. They soon discovered that the church was in danger of being split because of trouble over some property disputes between the three clans which constituted the village. One side would refuse to meet the missionary while the other side was present, and each hoped that the missionary would decide the matter in its favor. Efforts to settle the dispute proved fruitless. The matter was taken before the heathen official for settlement but with tragic results for all concerned. Realizing the seriousness of the situation, the missionaries decided to stay on for three months to conduct a Bible school and also sent an urgent request to their supporters in America to pray for the work at Three Clans.

At the end of three months of Bible school, there seemed to be an epidemic of quarrels and fleshly manifestations that seemed to betoken that the study had produced no results. But during the last two days of the missionaries' stay there, without any explanation that the missionaries could detect, a sudden and astonishing change took place. The atmosphere of the village was softening. At the closing night service a remarkable change came over the group. Men who had not spoken to each other for a long time, stood up, confessed their sins, and shook hands. Long-time enemies were reconciled, and the church was reunited in the Spirit of Christ. That night, after the missionaries had returned to their shanty, Mrs. Kuhn said to her husband, "John, I'm going to note this date down and see–I'm sure some one in the homeland has been very specially praying for us."

Two months passed. Then one day there arrived a letter from a prayer warrior in a small town in North America. This woman wrote that on that day she had been so burdened for the church at Three Clans that she could not do her housework. Finally she decided to call another lady who said that she had felt the same way. Together they decided to call a third lady and all went to prayer, each in her own kitchen. They spent the morning in intercession for those quarreling tribes at Three Clans. The letter closed by saying, "We feel that God has answered. You will know." When Mrs. Kuhn consulted her diary for the date mentioned in the letter, she found that it was during the same twenty-four hours in which the remarkable change had come over the church in Three Clans.

Those prayer warriors were not of earth's mighty ones. One of them was a woman with a serious heart condition. Another was expecting a serious operation, and the third was going blind. All three were elderly women, too physically frail to cross the small town and gather in one place, but each in her own kitchen was joined to the others in spirit, and a great victory was won through their united intercession.

V. *Through Prayer the Word is Spread and Glorified.*

Finally, brethren, pray for us, that the word of the Lord may have free course, and be glorified, even as it is with you.
(II Thess. 3:1)

Here again the Apostle Paul is requesting the prayers of his converts and indicating the contemplated results. They are to center their prayers on the missionaries with the anticipated result that through their work God's Word "may have free course"–may run and make a swift advance–and may "be glorified"–may be esteemed and accorded proper honor when men observe its transforming power in the lives of believers.

Paul was keenly aware of the need for the supporting prayers of God's people if the Word of God is to be preached with continuing effectiveness. He well knew that the effective efforts of godly and devout missionaries need the sustaining power of the intercessory prayers of the home church. Faithful intercession at home is the secret of success on the mission field.

J. Hudson Taylor, founder of the China Inland Mission, noticed the wonderful work of grace in connection with one of the stations of the mission. The number and spiritual character of the converts there had been far greater than at other stations, although the consecration of the missionaries at the other stations had been just as great as that of the more fruitful place. This situation remained a mystery to Hudson Taylor until, on a visit to England, he discovered the secret. At the close of one of his addresses, a man from the audience came forward to make his acquaintance. In the conversation which followed, Taylor was surprised at the accurate knowledge the man possessed concerning the fruitful mission station.

"But how is it," Taylor asked, "that you are so conversant with the conditions of that work?"

"Oh," he replied, "the missionary there and I are old college mates, and for years we have regularly corresponded. He has sent me names of inquirers and converts, and these I have daily taken to God in prayer."

At last the secret was found: a praying man at home daily and definitely interceding for specific cases on the field! This man had become a real intercessory missionary. How different the record of missionary service might be if more men like that could be found, men holding up the hands of the missionary on the field in definite, persistent intercessory prayer.

VI. *Through Prayer the Powers in Opposition to God Are Broken.*

Finally, brethren, pray for us . . . that we may be delivered from unreasonable and wicked men: for all men have not faith.
(II Thess. 3:1-2)

Paul knew from experience the dangers that threatened him and his work at the hands of wicked and unbelieving men. He asked the Thessalonians to pray specifically that he might be delivered from such men. He keenly felt the need for their prayers that the opposition might be successfully overcome. He knew that behind the human enemies were the forces of satanic wickedness.

When Nehemiah came to Jerusalem and began to rebuild the walls of the city, he encountered the fierce opposition of Sanballat and Tobiah. Every attempt was made to hinder the work, but the opposition was successfully defeated through constant prayer and diligent work (Neh. 4). Christian workers today, as in the days of Nehemiah, find that the enemies are fierce and determined and can be overcome only through persistent prayer. The battle may often be intense and prolonged, requiring the united prayers and efforts of God's children, but through persevering prayer God will give the victory.

A. C. Dixon tells us of being invited to preach in a certain college on Thanksgiving Day. The president of the school had written him that all but two or three members of the senior class were unsaved and that the school wanted him to come to preach for salvation, that these bright young men might not be sent out into the world unsaved.

When his train arrived Dr. Dixon found the president walking up and down on the platform in a nervous frame of mind. Taking his hand, he told Dr. Dixon that he had not slept that night because he had learned that there was a conspiracy led by the senior class against the services that day. The ringleaders had persuaded the other students in the college to pledge not to be influenced by anything the preacher said. Dr. Dixon admitted that it looked dark, but the president said, "If God Almighty does not come in, we are surely beaten but some of us have been praying, and I believe He will come to our help."

That morning when Dr. Dixon preached it felt to him like throwing a rubber ball against a granite wall. The students sat in groups nudging each other, as hard as stone. When he made an appeal at the close and asked who would like to decide for Christ and would like for him to pray for them, just one little fellow stood up right in front of him. He lived out in the village and was so insignificant that the ringleaders had forgotten to take him in on the conspiracy.

That afternoon there was a prayer meeting led by the president with the Christian students. Says Dr. Dixon, "I never heard such prayers in any other college, such broken-hearted petitions, and such a realization of weakness and dependence upon God. Somehow I felt when I went out from the prayer meeting, which had lasted for an hour and a half, that God was going to work."

That evening Dr. Dixon felt more liberty in preaching, but they had caught the little fellow and he was at the back among the conspirators, looking big in his own estimation now that he was included among those who opposed the whole movement. When the appeal was made there was not a single response. The benediction was pronounced and the audience quietly arose and went out.

Dr. Dixon found the president in the midst of a group of the teachers, and they were still praying. Tears coursed down the president's cheeks as he was praying that somehow God would touch the hearts of that senior class and the other students in the school. They remained there in prayer for five or ten minutes when the door opened, and one of the young men came awkwardly in and said, "Can I say a word, sir?" Dr. Dixon lifted his head, and the student continued, "When I got out of the door of the service hall, that covenant with hell was broken, and I have come to ask you to pray for me, as I would like to be a Christian."

While they were pointing him to Christ, the door opened again, and another student entered; then another came. They stayed there until one o'clock in the morning. Before they left that room, every unsaved student in the college except two had come in and asked for prayer and had accepted Christ.[5]

VII. *Through Prayer God's Servants Are Kept from Harm.*

Peter therefore was kept in prison: but prayer was made without ceasing of the church unto God for him. . . . But he, beckoning unto them with the hand to hold their peace, declared unto them how the Lord had brought him out of the prison. (Acts 12:5, 17)

The story of the miraculous deliverance of the Apostle Peter from the hand of King Herod Agrippa I is a dramatic instance of divine intervention on behalf of His servants when His people unite in intercessory prayer. But God does not always act in such a spectacular way in answering prayers for the safety of His servants. Before going to Jerusalem with the offering for the Judean saints, Paul wrote to the Christians in Rome and asked them to "strive together with me in your prayers to God for me; that I may be delivered from them that do not believe in Judea" (Rom. 15:30-31). But in Jerusalem a Jewish mob attacked and nearly killed Paul. God, however, used a Roman officer to rescue the apostle from death, and He gave Paul the assurance that he would get to Rome (Acts 21:27–23:11). Although Paul remained a prisoner for some four years, God overruled the events to bring a greater blessing out of them for the whole Church.

At other times God in His wisdom does not deliver His servants from danger, or even death. Peter was miraculously delivered, but James was slain (Acts 12). We may not understand when He permits someone like James to be suddenly and swiftly removed, whom we think cannot be spared on earth. But being confident that God does all things well, we can rest assured that in that day when we shall know even as we are known (I Cor. 13:12), the dark mysteries of God's providential dealing will be made plain to us.

Yet there is abundant evidence both in Scripture and missionary biography that God often works in a marvelous way for the physical safety of His servants in time of need. One such remarkable experience of deliverance is related by Mrs. Ruth Stull.[6] The Stulls were missionaries to the Indians in the Amazon jungles of Peru. One morning Mrs. Stull learned of an Indian woman who was seriously ill, and with another missionary couple she decided to go to the hut and help in order to reach her with the gospel. In a dugout they made their way upstream to the place where the path led to the Indian camp. They tied the boat at the bank and went to the camp. After working with the sick woman for two hours, they returned to the river to discover that it had been transformed into a raging torrent during their absence. The rains in the Andean mountains had melted the snows and suddenly flooded the river. They waded in to get their boat and started down the river.

The current caught the boat and threw it with terrific force against a large tree trunk which had toppled into the river. The impact threw Mrs. Stull across the fallen trunk into the churning river on the other side. As she struggled at the bottom of the river, Mrs. Stull found herself recalling with frightening clarity of mind how—because of the river's heavy undercurrent—few people who had fallen in had ever been rescued. Entangled in the vines that had been on the fallen tree, she realized that she was hopelessly lost.

Suddenly she found her head above the surface of the water. The boat had been paddled around the debris and was near the spot where she had disappeared. She got her hands on the boat, climbed back in, and they went on downstream. Aside from a great trembling which shook her body, Mrs. Stull felt no bad results from the strange experience.

When she and the other missionary couple arrived at the embankment upon which their house was located, they were met by her husband, asking if she were all right. Upon reaching their house her husband told her that while she was gone he had felt a definite urge to go into the house and pray, not for the sick woman, but for her. Says Mrs. Stull, "I have often thought what the result might have been had he put it off until the finishing of his task, or until the time of regular prayer. But he prayed, and I was saved."

Some weeks after that experience Mrs. Stull received a letter from a woman telling how two women's prayer groups had met for a joint prayer service. In the course of the meeting, one of the women related how she had been awakened in the night and impressed to get up and pray for Mrs. Stull, although she did not know Mrs. Stull personally. Another woman arose and said, "How strange. I was at my washer when the Spirit said to me, 'Pray for Mrs. Stull.' I turned off the current, and a prayer was literally poured through my heart for Mrs. Stull. But," she continued, "I do not know Mrs. Stull." The testimonies continued until more than twelve had declared that Mrs. Stull's name had been given to them with a definite call to pray during the past three weeks. When these women read in their denominational paper Mrs. Stull's account of her experience in the river, they noticed that the date on which the experience took place was the last day any one of them had received a special call to pray for Mrs. Stull.

VIII. *Through Prayer Mighty Works Are Accomplished.*

Verily, verily, I say unto you, He that believeth on me, the works that I do shall he do also; and greater works than these shall he do; because I go unto my Father. And whatsoever ye shall ask in my name, that will I do, that the Father may be glorified in the Son. (John 14:12-13)

The "greater works" promised to the believer by our Lord Himself are works of prayer grounded in the fact of the victory of the ascended Christ. These works are promised to those who will pray in harmony with the revelation given in Christ Jesus. Asking "in His name" is praying according to His revealed will. Such prayer has the promise of accomplishing mighty works.

In 1872 D. L. Moody made a short trip to England for rest, having no intention of preaching while there.[7] While he was in London, however, a Congregationalist minister asked him to preach in his church. Moody consented. The Sunday morning service was marked by smug, stolid drowsiness, making Moody rue his acceptance of the invitation. Following his message in the evening service when Moody asked all those who would decide for Christ to rise, hundreds did so. He was surprised, and thinking that they had misunderstood him, asked them to be seated. He repeated his invitation more clearly and again hundreds stood. As a result of the meetings which followed, that church received four hundred new people into its membership.

Moody began to make inquiries as to the secret. Finally he learned of a bedridden girl, a member of that church, named Marianne Adlard, who had prayed that God would send Moody to her church for a revival. She had read of his work in Chicago and, putting that report under her pillow, began to pray that God would send him to their church in London. When her older sister returned from the morning service and told her that a man named Moody from Chicago had preached that morning, the girl knew that her prayers were being answered. Moody visited her, and she asked him to write his name in her birthday book, promising that she would pray for him every day.

Some years later G. Campbell Morgan became pastor of the church where Marianne Adlard was a member.[8] Before leaving England for America in 1901, Dr. Morgan went to see her. She said to him, "I want you to reach that birthday book." He did so, and turning to February 5, he saw in Moody's familiar handwriting the words "D. L. Moody, Psalm 91." She said to him, "He wrote that for me when he came to see me in 1872, and I prayed for him every day till he went home to God." Then she continued, "Now, will you write your name on your birthday page, and let me pray for you until either you or I go home." Says Dr. Morgan, "I shall never forget writing my name in that book. To me the room was full of the Presence."

Prayer is asking divine omnipotence to work through yielded human weakness. God is looking for faithful intercessors through whose prayers He can perform more of the mighty works promised by our Lord. Truly prayer is the most powerful ministry which God has entrusted to His saints.

> More things are wrought by prayer
> Than this world dreams of. Wherefore, let thy voice
> Rise like a fountain for me night and day.
> For what are men better than sheep or goats
> That nourish a blind life within the brain,
> If, knowing God, they lift not hands of prayer

Both for themselves and those who call them friend?
For so the whole round earth is every way
Bound by gold chains about the feet of God.

–Alfred, Lord Tennyson.[9]

Notes

[1]Paul E. Billheimer, *Destined for the Throne* (Fort Washington, Pa.: Christian Literature Crusade, 1975), p. 17.

[2]Roger Martin, *R. A. Torrey, Apostle of Certainty* (Murfreesboro, Tenn.: Sword of the Lord Publishers, 1976), pp. 131-33.

[3]Rosalind Goforth, *How I Know God Answers Prayer* (Grand Rapids: Zondervan, 1921), pp. 15-16, 28-30.

[4]Isobel Kuhn, *Nests Above the Abyss* (Philadelphia: China Inland Mission, 1947), pp. 208-12; 217-23.

[5]A. C. Dixon, "Prayer and Revival," in *The Sword of the Lord,* 23 December 1949, pp. 1, 5.

[6]Ruth Stull, *Service on the Trail* (Philadelphia: Morning Cheer Book Store, 1944), pp. 36-46.

[7]J. C. Pollock, *Moody: A Biographical Portrait* (New York: The Macmillian Co., 1963), pp. 98-100.

[8]G. Campbell Morgan, *The Practice of Prayer* (New York: Revell,1906), pp. 126-27. This volume is dedicated to Marianne Adlard.

[9]"Morte D'Arthur," in *The Poetical Works of Alfred, Lord Tennyson* (London: Wark, Lock & Co., n.d.), p. 81.

III

Prayer-Sent Laborers

Then saith he unto his disciples, The harvest truly is plenteous, but the labourers are few; pray ye therefore the Lord of the harvest, that he will send forth labourers into his harvest. (Matt. 9:37-38)

The labor supply available for the Lord's harvest depends on the prayers of the people of God. The need for laborers constitutes an urgent call for intercession. These words from the lips of our Lord to His disciples challenge us to recognize these truths.

When Jesus uttered this statement, He was engaged in one of His evangelistic campaigns throughout the province of Galilee. It brought Him into contact with all sorts and conditions of people. In seeking to reach them with His message, Jesus used the threefold method of teaching, preaching, and healing (v. 35). He thus made a complete and balanced approach to the entire personality.

In spite of the intensity of His labors, multitudes of people in Galilee still remained unreached. The sight of these needy, neglected masses deeply touched and stirred His sensitive heart. His compassion and concern for these untended, weary, and forlorn flocks revealed Him to be the true Shepherd of Israel, as pictured by the prophet Ezekiel (chap. 34). Instead of exploiting the helpless flock, as did the false shepherds, He was burdened at their distressing circumstances. He felt deeply for them and was eager to help them. As the Good Shepherd, He came ''to seek and to save that which was lost'' (Luke 19:10).

But it was not enough that the Master be moved with compassion at the sight of those in need; the disciples too must be aroused to a realization of the desperate situation. They too must share the burden with Him. Christ accordingly turned to His disciples with His profound utterance: ''The harvest truly is plenteous, but the labourers are few; pray ye therefore the Lord of the harvest, that he will send forth labourers into his harvest'' (Matt. 9:37-38).

Today the risen Christ still seeks to direct the attention of His disciples to the masses of fatigued and forlorn humanity with their unmet needs. He is still seeking to stir their hearts with a sense of genuine compassion for the lost. How His people today need a sweeping revival of soul-stirring concern for those without Christ! Cries of crushing need keep crashing in on us today through television, radio, and print journalism. Who can fail to be aware of these appalling needs?

We are thankful for every evidence of concern for a needy world among believers today. We are moved at the physical sufferings of the unfortunate victims of cruel injustices and oppression, and rightly so. But how often are our souls stirred by a clear realization of the spiritual destitution of a sin-blighted world? May the Holy Spirit quicken in us a heartfelt concern as we contemplate the challenging words of our Lord.

I. *An Arousing Declaration*

Christ's declaration ''The harvest truly is plenteous'' forcefully drew the attention of His disciples to the situation. Jesus was thinking of the masses of people in Galilee who had not yet heard, much less received, His saving message. The people of Galilee, an immense multitude of some three million people, resided in some two hundred cities and villages. His ministry as yet had extended into only a comparatively few of these places. He could truly declare, ''The harvest is plenteous.'' In the original no verb is used: ''The harvest–plenteous!'' The form conveys the blunt reality.[1]

Jesus viewed these teeming multitudes as a harvest for God. The change from the figure of the shepherdless sheep to the waiting harvest aptly brings out the truth that the situation calls for the immediate cooperative action of the disciples. He did not say, ''The *field* is large,'' as though calling upon His disciples to till and sow it in preparation for a future harvest. Rather, they must recognize that the challenging harvest already lies before them, ready to be reaped.

Jesus saw in the huge crowds an inviting harvest for God. What do we see in the thronging masses around us? We will see very largely what we are looking for. The keen businessman sees in the crowds an inviting commercial harvest for rich financial gain. The demagogue discerns in the crowds his opportunity to promote his personal power and self-aggrandizement. The forces of sin and lawlessness find the crowds an inviting harvest for sinful exploitation. What do you see?

Years ago an evangelist and the owner of a city street car company were riding down the street together in an automobile. A streetcar, loaded to capacity, turned the corner and came toward them. "Look," cried the owner, "a carload of nickels."

"A carload of nickels?" replied the evangelist. "I was thinking, a carload of eternity-bound souls."

Which do we see? Are our eyes opened to the potential spiritual harvest for God in the masses around us? If we had spiritually opened eyes to see the harvest, would not our hearts too be stirred with compassion?

II. *A Sad Admission*

The statement "but the labourers are few" sets this further fact in contrast to the vastness of the waiting harvest. Our Lord's vision of the needs of the masses around Him brought into sharp focus the dire need for more laborers. The reality saddened His yearning heart. But His disciples also must come to realize the sad fact.

There were numerous workers in that day who were zealously at work for themselves and their party. The Pharisees made strenuous efforts to win others to their sect. Jesus recognized their zeal but lamented the perverted purposes that dominated their activities. He said to them, "Ye compass sea and land to make one proselyte, and when he is made, ye make him twofold more the child of hell than yourselves" (Matt. 23:15). Even so today there are many laborers abroad in the fields avidly gathering the ripened harvest for perverted ends. And, sadly enough, their zeal and skill seem often to exceed that of the true laborers for Christ.

The scarcity of the laborers, in view of the vastness of the harvest, created an appalling situation. It disturbed and saddened the heart of Jesus, for He well understood the tragedy of an unreaped harvest.

A missionary in Palestine recounts that one day on a journey he came past a field of grain totally white. He asked a companion what it was. "A field of wheat," was the reply. "But why is it so white?" he inquired. "It is overripe," was the response. "There are not enough men around here to cut it, and it has been left too long. Unless it is cut at once, the owner will get no harvest, for the birds will eat much of it, and the rest will fall to the ground and be lost." And even as the words were spoken, from two different directions came large flocks of birds and settled on the field to enjoy the feast so temptingly spread before them. Are we aware of the birds of prey swooping down on God's harvest today?

These two concise statements of Jesus, producing a stark contrast, paint a disquieting scene which the disciples could not ignore. His words could not fail to stir them and stimulate their desire to respond to the need. Even so today, should not His words stab our consciences and shake us out of our spiritual lethargy?

III. *A Call for Intercession*

In view of the tremendous need, we are made to ask, "Lord, what do you want me to do?" As though in answer to this query in the hearts of the disciples, the Lord points out the appropriate response by calling for definite intercession. "Pray ye therefore the Lord of the harvest, that he will send forth labourers into his harvest" (v. 38). After we have seen the need, the Master desires that our initial response be to pray for laborers. His words contain a number of important truths concerning intercessory prayer.

1. The words reveal *the inducement* for intercessory prayer. "Pray ye therefore"–because of the vastness of the harvest and the scarcity of the laborers. A vital apprehension of these two facts inevitably leads to a heartfelt concern that finds expression in earnest intercession. As long as our hearts remain cold and indifferent to these conditions, we will remain prayerless. A major reason for the lack of intercessory prayer is the prevailing lack of a compelling realization of the lostness of the unsaved.

2. When seen in their context, these words reveal *the primacy* of intercessory prayer in Christian service. Jesus points to intercessory prayer as the resource available to meet the desperate need for workers. Following this call for prayer, the Lord Jesus carefully instructed, empowered, and sent forth the Twelve. But before they were ready to be sent as His messengers, they needed

to be trained in the school of prayer. His order is first prayer, then service; nay rather, prayer is the first and primary form of service.

It is essential that we retain this order of prayer followed by service. This order was vital in the thought of our Lord, for in connection with His sending out the seventy, we again have the same order (Luke 10:1-3). Likewise the apostles observed this order in the early church (Acts 6:4). With our modern emphasis on Christian service, we are in danger of leading young believers to launch out into active service before they have learned to know the place and importance of prayer in the Lord's work. We need to urge all believers to engage in Christian service, but such service is often ineffectual because we have neglected to emphasize the primacy of prayer in a life of Christian service. Ryle urgently pleads, "Never, never may we forget that if we would do good to the world, our first duty is to pray!"[2] When prayer is given first place in our lives, our service will not thereby be minimized or neglected, but it will rather be made truly effective.

3. Intercessory prayer is to be *directed to* "the Lord of the harvest." The Lord is the owner of the harvest and He is concerned about it. He uses men to do the harvesting, but the work is His. The worker must submit to the sovereignty of God in the selection of the laborers and their appointment to their appropriate sphere of service. He must send forth and direct the work of the harvesters if it is to be fruitful for God. Self-appointed workers in self-selected fields with self-chosen methods and self-determined aims do more harm than good. Jesus did not ask the disciples to go out and find the needed laborers, but He did ask them to pray that the Lord of the harvest would send forth the needed workers.

4. *The request* to be made is that God will "send forth labourers." The great need for workers must elicit the specific prayer request that God will provide the workers. The word used in the original is very expressive, "that he may *thrust forth* labourers." It is the same term rendered "put forth" in Matthew 9:25 and "cast out" in verses 33-34. Broadus observes that the term "always implies urgency, haste, constraint," while the aorist tense used here means "that the laborers should be sent out promptly, pushed into their work."[3] Violence is not implied here, but the term denotes the divine compulsion upon human lives that makes them willing to leave the comforts of home and go into the darkness of heathendom with the message of salvation.

Only the power of God can push out the needed workers into the harvest field.

James H. McConkey gives an illustration from the life of P. Cameron Scott, founder of the African Inland Mission, of this power of God in thrusting forth a worker.[4] For several years this young man drifted along upon the listless tide of a shallow Christian life, seemingly without a thought of God's claim upon him. Then there came a time when the Holy Spirit began to work mightily in his heart to induce him to surrender his life. Again and again the Spirit moved and troubled him with the words of the text "Ye are not your own . . . for ye are bought with a price" (I Cor. 6:19-20). He could not get away from those words; they so troubled his resisting heart that in desperation he sought to erase the text from his Bible, but that did not help. Finally he yielded himself to the call of the Spirit, and his life of surrender to God left untold blessings in its train.

This work of thrusting forth laborers into the harvest must not be limited to the calling of ministers and missionaries. God has a place for every member of His Church in the reaping of the whitened fields. God likewise takes lay members of His Church, engaged in the common tasks of life, and "sets them on fire" for Him, mightily using them in the bringing in of the harvest. Every believer, humbly faithful as a witness for God in his daily life, can have a share in the gathering of the sheaves for the Lord.

5. The words of our Lord indicate *the duty* of intercessory prayer. "*Pray ye* therefore" is a command from our Lord Himself and carries the same binding obligation of any other command. God's people are under solemn obligation to pray for the needed workers. How often this need for workers is publicly discussed and lamented; committees are appointed to investigate and report; yet how little believing prayer there is for the needed workers. The Church must grasp–and practice–the solemn truth that her Lord holds her responsible to pray for the needed laborers.

A chapter out of the history of the early Moravian church offers a clear testimony to the power of intercessory prayer in meeting the needs for laborers. In 1727 at Herrnhut there was begun a continuing prayer vigil which went on for one hundred years.

> It was known as the 'Hourly Intercession,' and it meant that by relays of brethren and sisters prayer without ceasing was made to God for all the work and wants of His Church. In this case it

kindled a burning desire to make Christ's salvation known to the heathen. It led to the beginning of modern foreign missions. From that one small village community more than one hundred missionaries went out in twenty-five years.[5]

In view of the fact that our Master has commanded such an intercessory prayer ministry and that history demonstrates the results of faithful obedience to the command, how tragic that believers as a whole have not more fully entered into this ministry. One of the major sins of the Christian Church today is its prayerlessness.

6. The words of our Lord in the original also convey the thought of *urgency* in intercessory prayer. The command "Pray ye" in the aorist tense has in it a sense of urgency, setting forth a duty that must be obeyed at once. A realization of the desperate need for such prayer will create an urgency in our praying. Effective prayer arises out of a burden for a need to be met, be that need our own or that of others. Whenever this consciousness of a pressing need is lacking, prayer tends to become formal and powerless. Prayer arises spontaneously from a burdened heart.

Whenever the Holy Spirit places in our hearts the urge to pray, how important it is that we obey! Such Spirit-prompted prayer is in accordance with the will of God. To quench such a call to prayer will have an adverse impact upon our own spiritual life. Watchman Nee testifies:

> If you do not pray, you will feel suffocated within as if there is something left undone. In the event you still do not pray, you will feel even more weighed down. Finally, if you do not pray at all, the spirit of prayer as well as the burden of prayer will be so dulled that it will be difficult for you to regain such feeling and to pray the prayer according to God's will afterwards.[6]

7. These words also contain an intimation of the marvelous *privilege* of prayer. We are asked to pray for workers in order that God may meet the need by sending out the needed laborers. The eternal God could send forth workers without our prayers, but He has chosen to relate His working with our asking. In furthering the work of His kingdom, God desires not to work independently but to have His people cooperate with Him. He works to communicate His will to His people and then delights to answer their prayer for its fulfillment. He has thus provided for each of His children the glorious opportunity of working with Him in the fulfillment of His

purposes. Each may have a share in the work of gathering in the harvest through the hidden ministry of intercession. "Prayer is indeed a power on which the ingathering of the harvest and the coming of the kingdom do in very truth depend."[7]

In view of the explicit command of our Lord to pray for laborers and the realization that God assuredly works in response to such prayers, we must humbly confess that we have not adequately entered into this glorious privilege of working by prayer. Acknowledging and confessing our sin, let us resolve to be obedient to this urgent call to pray for the needed laborers to gather in the whitened harvest for our Lord and Saviour. May we too hear in our hearts the call of the Spirit and say with the poet:

A call to prayer! I cannot sleep!
A midnight vigil I must keep!
For God doth call; I hear Him speak:
"To prayer! To prayer! (I but repeat)
To prayer! To prayer! Prevailing prayer!"
The need of such is everywhere;
It covers earth—it fills the air—
This urgent need of urgent prayer!

To bended knee! To bended knee!
God's call to you—God's call to me;
Because what is, and what's to be
Shall reach throughout eternity.
Like Christ our Lord—like unto Him
In whom was found no guile—no sin,
Who "prayed all night." And we His kin
Should pray—yes pray, like unto Him.

O friends, I say—again I say,
This truth has gripped my heart this day:
The Need of Prayer! Let come what may,
We will prevail! Oh, "Watch and pray"!
Awake! Awake! Ye saints awake!
Stand in the breach for Jesus' sake—
Our God the powers of hell shall break!

—Author Unknown

Notes

[1]"Truly" is not represented in the original. The Greek term *men,* with the following *de,* simply indicates that this clause stands in contrast to the next clause. The rendering "truly" was first introduced into the English text in the Great Bible, which appeared in 1539, and was retained in the King James Version.

[2]J. C. Ryle, *Expository Thoughts on the Gospels,* vol. 1, *Matthew–Mark* (Reprint ed., Grand Rapids: Zondervan, 1956), p. 94.

[3]John A. Broadus, *Commentary on the Gospel of Matthew* (1886; reprint ed., Grand Rapids: Kregel, 1990), p. 212.

[4]James H. McConkey, *The Surrendered Life* (Pittsburgh, Pa.: Silver Pub. Society, 1927), pp. 73-77.

[5]John Greenfield, *Power from on High* (Atlantic City, N.J.: The World Wide Revival Prayer Movement, 1931), pp. 29-30.

[6]Watchman Nee, *Let Us Pray* (New York: Christian Fellowship Publishers, 1977), p. 34.

[7]Andrew Murray, *With Christ in The School of Prayer* (New York: Grosset and Dunlap, n.d.), p. 58.

IV

The Prayer Ministry of the Church

I exhort therefore, that, first of all, supplications, prayers, intercessions, and giving of thanks, be made for all men; for kings, and for all that are in authority; that we may lead a quiet and peaceable life in all godliness and honesty. For this is good and acceptable in the sight of God our Saviour; who will have all men to be saved, and to come unto the knowledge of the truth. (I Tim. 2:1-4)

The ministry of prayer is the most important service in which the Church of Christ can engage. It is a service in accordance with God's will, pleasing in His sight, urged upon the assemblies of His people, and productive of immeasurable good. The passage quoted above is a clarion call to the Church to engage in world-wide prayer. Such praying is the lifeblood of Christian worship.

In I Timothy 2, Paul is speaking about the place of prayer in the public services of the Christian congregation. The passage conveys God's desire for His Church in every age and every region. The verses quoted above convey five aspects of this prayer ministry.

I. *The Importance of the Prayer Ministry*

Deeply convinced of the need of such a prayer ministry on the part of the Church, the apostle begins by urging its practice as being of primary importance. He writes, ''I exhort therefore, that, first of all, supplications, prayers, intercessions, and giving of thanks, be made'' (v. 1). The King James Version connects the words "first of all" with the making of supplications, and so on. That rendering would suggest that such intercessory prayers were to be the first thing in the order of worship in the local congregation. It is generally agreed, however, that the words should be connected with "exhort." They mark "not priority of time, but of dignity."[1] Paul is concerned to give the subject of prayer first place in importance and treatment. Other matters in connection with the worship services will follow.

The Greek word here translated "exhort" is the same term rendered "beseech" in Romans 12:1. In such connections it carries the meaning of "to beg, to entreat, to urge." The term basically denotes the concept of calling someone alongside for the purpose of urging him to consider an important matter. Paul's words here are not expressed as a command but form an appeal to the conscience and the desire of the readers to do what is appropriately asked of them. The practice of prayer cannot be forced by an outward command but must be prompted by an inner conviction of its importance and need. It is this inner conviction of its importance that the apostle seeks to stimulate.

The churches of Christ have generally failed to perceive the importance of the ministry of prayer here urged by Paul, nor have they adequately engaged in its practice. In many churches prayer has ceased to be a vital part of their public services. Even in the prayer meetings little time is devoted to actual prayer. Who can truly measure the opportunities to work by prayer thus being neglected? Who can comprehend the tragic loss of power to promote the work of the Lord thus being sustained? The churches of Christ have sinned in failing to pray as here directed! It is time to confess our failure with shame and contrition and ask the Lord for a heart of prayer and compassion.

> Oh, for a heart that is burdened,
>   Infused with a passion to pray.
> Oh, for a stirring within me,
>   Oh, for His power each day!

II. *The Nature of the Prayer Ministry*

The prayer ministry the apostle urges the Church to engage in is not discharged by an occasional prayer for all men. His use of the present tense indicates that it is to be the habitual, continued practice of the Church thus to pray. *The New Testament in Modern*

English well brings out the true force: "First of all then, I am urging that supplications, prayers, intercessions and thanksgiving be offered regularly for all men."[2]

Besides indicating that the praying is to be regularly engaged in, the apostle uses four different terms to set forth the comprehensive nature of this ministry: "supplications, prayers, intercessions, and giving of thanks." The four terms are, of course, not to be understood as indicating the successive elements in the worship liturgy of the Church. Nor do we accept the view that no distinctions in meaning are to be sought, as though the terms "are merely accumulated, like synonyms in legal documents, or various phrases in rhetorical addresses, to ensure completeness and to add force."[3] In view of the exact usage of words in the Scriptures, we cannot agree that Paul intended no distinctions of meaning in his use of these terms. While rejecting unwarranted distinctions between the terms, we are justified in seeing varied aspects of the prayers being offered. Bernard well notes that the different words used "point to different moods of the supplicant rather than to the different forms into which public prayer may be cast."[4]

1. "Supplications." This is a general word for prayer and means a request or a petition. As such it is used of petitions directed both to God and to men. Coming from a verb meaning to want or to lack, the word "signifies a prayer which springs from the feeling of want."[5] The basic thought thus conveyed by this term is that of prayer prompted by a conscious sense of need. It is prayer arising out of a sense of human inadequacy to meet the demand of life.

Such a conscious sense of need, either our own or another's, is essential to all effective praying. Without such a sense of need, our prayers lack depth and sincerity. Our prayers become formal, often the mere uttering of words that have lost their meaning and value for us. What believer has not at times found himself saying certain words in prayer, only to realize that his mind was on something far removed from his uttered words? When there is a real prayer burden arising out of a specific sense of need, it is not hard to concentrate on one's prayer. Surely in these eventful days when the pressing needs of mankind come crashing in upon us from every side, it is inexcusable to lack a motive for prayer.

Critical world needs, as well as local and personal needs, constitute a standing challenge to pray.

2. "Prayers." This is a general term used to include all the different kinds of prayer. It does not denote any restriction in contents, but, unlike the preceding term, it is used only of prayer to God. Like our English word *prayer,* it is a reverent term. True prayer must have in it the element of reverence for God. In approaching God, we need to remember that He is in heaven, holy and omnipotent, while we are but finite creatures of the dust. People who would not think of thoughtlessly rushing into the presence of royalty here on earth nevertheless often approach the King of kings in an irreverent and careless manner.

3. "Intercessions." The Greek term occurs only here and in I Timothy 4:5 in the New Testament. If the preceding word carries the thought of reverence, this word suggests the thought of child-like confidence in prayer. It comes from a Greek verb meaning "to fall in with, meeting with in order to converse freely." It thus conveys the thought of meeting another for the purpose of conversation, consultation, or supplication. Originally the term did not carry the thought of intercession, but in papyrus usage it acquired a technical meaning to denote a "petition" offered to a governor or a king. It contains the picture of a little boy who approaches his father with perfect confidence and freely tells him what he desires. Trench says that the word suggests "free familiar prayer, such as boldly draws near to God."[6] The leading thought in the term is that of boldness of access, or confidence in prayer (I John 5:14). The petitions expressed may be either for ourselves or for others. Hendriksen suggests that here the meaning is "pleading in the interest of others, and doing this without 'holding back' in any way."[7]

4. "Giving of thanks." This word indicates the spirit in which our prayers are to be offered. It is the spirit of gratitude to God for all the blessings that have already been received. The plural noun, "thanksgivings," denotes that Paul has in view not merely the inner attitude of gratitude but the repeated public expressions of thanksgiving to God for His blessings. Thanksgiving is the complement of all true prayer. It prepares the heart to appreciate properly the blessings yet to be received. But the context here makes clear that the thanksgiving is not to be limited to our own blessings but also includes gratitude to God for His gracious dealings in the lives of those for whom the Church prays.

III. *The Scope of the Prayer Ministry*

The scope of the praying being urged upon the Church is indicated in the words "for all men; for kings, and for all that are in authority."

1. "For all men." The prayer ministry of the Church is to be worldwide in its scope. Prayer in all the aspects indicated is to be made "for all men." How far this transcends the ordinary scope of the prayers heard in churches today! Seldom do the prayers of a local church reach beyond its local fellowship or denomination. Another testifies to this fact as follows:

> Very seldom, in large churches or in small churches, or even in spiritual churches, have I heard a prayer for all men. Those who pray scarcely reach further than their own churches. Some pray a little for the missionaries overseas; but if we could cover all men through our prayers, what might not happen.[8]

This exhortation to pray for all men is God's means of safeguarding His Church against self-centeredness. Believers are always prone to be so preoccupied with their own limited sphere of interests that their intercession tends to be confined to their own concerns. But the broader the scope of prayer, the larger becomes the spiritual vision of the soul. Such a catholicity of outlook in prayer fosters spiritual concern for a sin-darkened world. While maintaining its separation from the world, the Church that prays for all men is thus continually reminded of its commission to bring the message of salvation to all men.

All men need the prayers of the Church. All men are sinners and need prayer on their behalf. They may not pray for themselves; so the Church must pray for them so that none are unprayed for. Lenski remarks, "If such praying were useless, the apostle would not write what he here does write."[9] God works in the lives of men as His people pray; is not the tragic reality that so many remain spiritually unreached at least in part because the saints have not specifically prayed for them?

2. "For kings, and for all that are in authority." Because men live in national groupings, the Church must also pray for the rulers of the nations. Prayer is to be not only worldwide but also national and patriotic. Christians are to pray for the leaders of the nation in which they live. The plural "kings" is apparently used because Paul is thinking of the sovereign rulers as they succeed one another in the course of history. It was very obvious then, as

now, that the type of government believers live under profoundly influences their lives and activities. Ward observes that Paul instructs that prayer is to be made "*for* kings," not "to" them, and states the implication: "This is an implicit denial of Caesar worship. The emperor himself is under the law of God."[10]

Paul insists that prayer is also to be made for "all that are in authority," those in positions of governmental authority under the kings. Paul well knew that the attitude of such lesser officials could have a profound impact upon the churches in a local area. Such lesser authorities also needed the prayers of believers.

The prayers of the Church, however, are not to be limited to those who are good rulers. The Apostle Paul understood what it meant to pray for a wicked Nero. This practice of praying for the rulers was especially important for Christians in the early Church when their attitude to the state's religion exposed them to the suspicion of disloyalty. The Christian apologists frequently pointed to the prayers of the Christians for the reigning emperor. They maintained that the Christians proved their loyalty by their continued prayers for the emperor. And today, where believers live under democratic forms of government, "prayer for the government, rather than denunciation of it, is the more effective, as well as more befitting service in the Christian assembly."[11]

Paul does not limit these prayer activities in the assemblies to "those in authority *over us.*" The prayers of the Church for rulers are not to be limited to those in authority over their own land. The Church needs to pray explicitly for the rulers of other lands, even for those who are unfriendly, or openly hostile, toward Christianity. If the Church had been faithful in praying for those lands and their rulers, perhaps the course of events there would have been very different.

One summer day in 1910, Rev. E. Joseph Evans went with some companions for an outing in the Adirondack Mountains. His heart became burdened with a sense of need, and he retired into a quiet woodland retreat to meet his Lord. He began to pray, but the burden increased; he prayed for the usual objects of prayer, but the burden became more intense. Finally his prayers began to focus upon the person of Edward VII, the king of England. In deep agony and travail he pleaded for the salvation of the king's soul. Before the end of the day there was a lifting of spirit, with the gracious and sweet assurance that the king of England, far away across the Atlantic, had come to a saving knowledge of the Lord Jesus Christ.

On his return to the hotel he learned from his companions that the king of England had died that day. "I did not know he was ill," Evans replied.

"Neither did we, but there is word by cable that he just died."

"How wonderful, then," replied Evans, "to know that he has been redeemed by the precious blood of Christ."

"How do you know he was a believer?" he was asked.

"God gave me that assurance in the intercession of this day," was the simple reply.

Years later an English clergyman, Dr. J. Gregory Mantel, entertained Mr. Evans and Dr. V. R. Edman at dinner. In the course of the conversation Dr. Mantel said, entirely without question on the part of his visitors, "Have you heard how Edward VII came to the Saviour on the last day of his life?" Dr. Mantel went on to relate how the king had asked his lords-in-waiting to go down to Fleet Street to secure for him a copy of a tract which as a boy he had received from his godly mother, Queen Victoria. Long search was made, then a copy was found. It was read to the dying king, who recognized it as the very words that his mother had given him, and this brought him to full assurance of faith in Christ. Little was it realized that at that very time a young Welsh-American Christian, far away in the Adirondack Mountains of New York, was pleading for him before the throne of grace.

IV. *The Results of the Prayer Ministry*

Paul's further words, "that we may lead a quiet and peaceable life in all godliness and honesty" (v. 2b), indicate not the contents of the prayers to be offered but rather the contemplated result of such prayers. Van Oosterzee notes, "The Apostle does not mean that the church should be influenced, through such petitions, to lead a quiet and peaceable life under authority; but he supposes that God, who guides the hearts of kings as the waterbrooks (Prov. 21:1), will, in answer to the prayer of church, move the hearts of kings, and of all in authority, to leave Christians at rest."[12]

Paul believed that the faithful prayers of the Church would make a definite difference in national affairs. Paul believed that prayer changes things. He would have scorned the view which regards prayer as a subjective exercise which influences only the one who prays.

To say that this is a selfish prayer is to miss the point. The blessings contemplated as wrought by the prayers of the Church are by no means limited to the praying believers. The entire nation profits by the conditions here envisioned. The ultimate purpose, however, is the salvation of souls, as verse 4 indicates.

The realization of this soul-saving purpose demands that believers live "a quiet and peaceable life in all godliness and honesty." The two adjectives, "quiet and peaceable," describe the kind of life that will be possible because of their prayers. Vincent points out that of the two Greek words so rendered, the former "denotes quiet arising from the absence of outward disturbances," while the latter denotes "tranquility arising from within."[13] They thus describe conditions free from outward harassment and inner fears. Knowing that peace of heart which comes through justification by faith (Rom. 5:1), the believer will seek profitably to use the conditions of outward peace to present to his fellow men the gospel of peace.

The task of proclaiming the gospel of peace makes its demands upon the life of the messenger. He must lead a life characterized by "all godliness and honesty." "Godliness" stands first as indicating its Godward character. His life is reverent and respectful, dominated by "the fear of the Lord." The second term, rendered "honesty" in the KJV, has reference to his relations to men. The original word is more adequately rendered by "gravity"; it connotes an attitude of moral earnestness which is reflected in a dignified and worthy conduct toward men so as to command their respect. The word "all" is best constructed with both nouns and indicates that both features are to be fully displayed in the believer. If believers were always exemplifying such character, the salvation of souls would be greatly furthered.

V. *The Basis of the Prayer Ministry*

In verses 3 and 4 the apostle indicates why each local church should pray in this way. Each should do so not merely because Paul says so. There are weightier considerations. Paul desires to help them grasp the full import of this matter and to foster such praying. It is one thing to know the importance of intercessory prayer; it is another thing to practice it consistently.

1. "For this is good." Taken alone, these words mark the intrinsic excellence of such praying. It is quite possible to connect these words with the following adjective and read them as one

thought, namely, God's evaluation of such prayer. It seems better, however, with most commentators, to regard these words as an independent thought. Van Oosterzee comments, "Every such prayer is good in and for itself; it shows the true Christian spirit which marks the professor of the gospel; it yields us the enjoyment of that privilege named in verse 2."[14] The Berkeley Version suggestively renders this passage "Such praying is wholesome."[15]

A missionary couple, in charge of ten stations, felt constrained to write to the secretary of their mission board confessing that there seemed to be no progress whatever in their stations. Because of indifference, opposition, and ignorance, they had made no headway. Conditions seemed hopeless to human eyes. The missionaries suggested to the secretary that he try to find ten people who would each make one of these stations his or her prayer object and pray unceasingly for the work of the Lord there.

Time passed and things began to happen in seven of the stations. Revival broke out. The people gladly received the gospel, and great numbers flocked into the churches. But in the other three stations there was no change. Again the missionaries wrote to the secretary describing what was happening in seven of the stations and expressing their anxiety concerning the other three. They asked if he could suggest any explanation. It was not difficult for the secretary to make clear the seeming mystery. He had succeeded in getting seven people to pray for the seven stations where God was graciously giving revival blessings, but he had not found any one for the other three stations.

2. "And acceptable in the sight of God." The thought here reaches much higher than the merely pragmatic. Such praying is acceptable before God because it is in accord with His will for all mankind. For the child of God this should ever be the chief motive for engaging in this ministry of prayer. Verse 4 suggests that God's purpose for men is twofold.

There is, first, His *saving purpose* for mankind. Paul says that "God our Saviour . . . will have all men to be saved." Such praying is "acceptable," or pleasing, to God because it is in accord with His desire for the salvation of mankind.

God desires the salvation of all men, and all men are rendered savable through Christ "who gave himself a ransom for all" (v. 6). Yet God has declared that men must be saved through the ordained way of faith in Christ. That many are not saved is due, not to any inadequacy in God's provision for man's salvation, but to man's rejection of the specific means of salvation which God has been pleased to appoint. As Ellicott says, "Redemption is universal, yet conditional; all may be saved, yet all will not be saved, because all will not conform to God's appointed way."[16] The resultant favorable conditions flowing from the praying of the Church will offer believers greater opportunities to lead the unsaved to accept God's way of salvation.

There is furthermore God's purpose that men should "come unto *the knowledge of* the *truth*." This may be regarded as the means of salvation, or it may be thought of as a further aspect of God's saving purpose. The latter seems preferable. It is true that man must have certain knowledge of the truth of the gospel to be saved; yet there remains much to be learned after he is saved. The Greek word for "knowledge" here used is not the simple word for knowledge but the compound form which seems to mean growing knowledge or perception. Williams accordingly renders the phrase "to come to an increasing knowledge of the truth."[17] Guthrie concludes that this phrase here means "the whole revelation of God in Christ, to know which must be the ultimate aim of Christian salvation."[18]

The tragic failure of many Christians to continue to grow in their experiential apprehension of the full truth in Christ Jesus is a definite hindrance to the cause of God. It was Paul's prayer for the Colossian Christians that they might continue "increasing in the knowledge of God" (Col. 1:10). Are we remaining spiritual dwarfs, or are we growing in our knowledge of the things of God as embodied in His inspired Word?

One neglected aspect of God's truth is the place that God has given to intercessory prayer in the furtherance of His kingdom. If all Christians would come into a full apprehension of this important truth and faithfully practice it, how it would speed the cause of Christ in the salvation of souls! Oh, that the churches of Christ might be awakened to a realization of their mighty opportunity to work for God through the united ministry of intercessory prayer! Here is a high and holy service which beckons to every child of God. Only eternity will reveal the impact of the faithful exercise of this ministry.

There's a holy, high vocation,
  Needing workers everywhere;
'Tis the highest form of service,
  'Tis the ministry of prayer.

No one need stand idly longing
  For a place in which to share
Active service for the Master,
  There is always room in prayer.

In these days of tribulation
  Wickedness pervades the air,
And the battles we engage in
  Must be won through fervent prayer.

There's no weapon half so mighty
  As the intercessors bear;
Nor a broader field of service
  Than the ministry of prayer.

Do you long to see the millions,
  Who are perishing today,
Snatched as brands plucked from the burning?
  Do you long, yet seldom pray?

Come and join the intercessors!
  Laurels, then, some day you'll wear;
For there is no higher service
  Than the ministry of prayer.

−Annie Lind Woodworth

Notes

[1]Charles J. Ellicott, *A Critical and Grammatical Commentary on the Pastoral Epistles* (Andover: Warren F. Draper, 1865), p. 42.

[2]Helen Barrett Montgomery, *The New Testament in Modern English* (Philadelphia: Judson Press, 1924).

[3]A. G. Hervey, et al., "I Timothy," in *The Pulpit Commentary* (Reprint ed., Chicago: Wilcox and Follett Co., n.d.), 21:32.

[4]J. H. Bernard, *The Pastoral Epistles,* Cambridge Greek Testament for Schools and Colleges (1899; reprint ed., Cambridge: University Press, 1922), p. 38.

[5]J. J. Van Oosterzee, "The Pastoral Letters," in *Lange's Commentary on the Holy Scriptures* (1863; reprint ed., Grand Rapids: Zondervan, n.d.), 22:28.

[6]Richard Chenevix Trench, *Synonyms of the New Testament* (1880; reprint ed., Grand Rapids: Eerdmans, 1947), p. 190.

[7]William Hendriksen, *Exposition of the Pastoral Epistles,* New Testament Commentary (Grand Rapids: Baker, 1957), p. 93.

[8]"Prayer That is Good in God's Sight," *The Prophetic Word,* November 1949, p. 614.

[9]R.C.H. Lenski, *The Interpretation of St. Paul's Epistles to the Colossians, to the Thessalonians, to Timothy, to Titus and to Philemon* (Columbus, Ohio: Lutheran Book Concern, 1937), p. 549.

[10]Ronald A. Ward, *Commentary on 1 & 2 Timothy & Titus* (Waco, Texas: Word Books, 1974), p. 44.

[11]H. Harvey, "Commentary on the Pastoral Epistles, First and Second Timothy and Titus; and the Epistle of Philemon," in *An American Commentary on the New Testament* (1890; reprint ed., Philadelphia: The American Baptist Pub. Society, n.d.), 6:30.

[12]Van Oosterzee, p. 28.

[13]Martin R. Vincent, *Word Studies in the New Testament* (1900; reprint ed., Grand Rapids: Eerdmans, 1946), 4:217.

[14]Van Oosterzee, p. 24.

[15]Gerrit Verkuyla, ed., *The Modern Language Bible, The New Berkeley Version* (Grand Rapids: Zondervan, 1969).

[16]Ellicott, p. 45.

[17]Charles B. Williams, *The New Testament, A Private Translation in the Language of the People* (1937; reprint ed., Chicago: Moody Press, 1949).

[18]Donald Guthrie, *The Pastoral Epistles,* The Tyndale New Testament Commentaries (Grand Rapids: Eerdmans, 1957), p. 72.

V

Empowerment Through Intercession

Then came Amalek, and fought with Israel in Rephidim. And Moses said unto Joshua, Choose us out men, and go out, fight with Amalek: to morrow I will stand on the top of the hill with the rod of God in mine hand.

So Joshua did as Moses had said to him, and fought with Amalek: and Moses, Aaron, and Hur went up to the top of the hill. And it came to pass, when Moses held up his hand, that Israel prevailed: and when he let down his hand, Amalek prevailed. But Moses' hands were heavy; and they took a stone, and put it under him, and he sat thereon; and Aaron and Hur stayed up his hands, the one on the one side, and the other on the other side; and his hands were steady until the going down of the sun. And Joshua discomfited Amalek and his people with the edge of the sword.

And the Lord said unto Moses, Write this for a memorial in a book, and rehearse it in the ears of Joshua: for I will utterly put out the remembrance of Amalek from under heaven. And Moses built an altar, and called the name of it Jehovah-nissi: For he said, Because the Lord hath sworn that the Lord will have war with Amalek from generation to generation. (Exod. 17:8-16)

Jehovah used the attack of Amalek on Israel, at the very beginning of its national history, to demonstrate to His chosen people the potency of intercession. The event reveals a mighty means of strength and victory which God has graciously afforded

His people in all ages. The experience of Israel in its conflict with Amalek affirms the reality of empowerment through intercession.

Like Israel of old, God's people today are engaged in fateful conflict with a powerful spiritual enemy. The picture of the Christian life as a battle has always appealed to believers because it is so true to our experience. In Ephesians 6 Paul depicts the Christian life as a spiritual conflict with spiritual wickedness and urges upon believers the need to appropriate the divine provision for empowerment. In this fierce struggle we could experience only defeat if we did not receive divine strengthening. The enemies being confronted are vicious and determined; victory is assured to God's people only as we appropriate the strength of the Lord for the battle.

Since the things that happened to Israel were "written for our admonition" (I Cor. 10:11), this record of the conflict between Israel and Amalek embodies vital lessons for us today.

I. *The Attack of Amalek* (v. 8)

The attack of Amalek was made while Israel was on its way to Mount Sinai. It was the first such attack upon them since their escape from Egypt. It probably occurred about two months after the exodus.

The Amalekites were the descendants of Amalek, the grandson of Esau (Gen. 36:12, 16). Although a part of the Edomite race, the Amalekites maintained a distinct identity as the most powerful nomadic tribe in the Sinai Peninsula. They were a fierce and warlike people, harboring a distinct hostility toward Israel. Balaam spoke of them as "the first of the nations" (Num. 24:20). Rawlinson thinks that "they were among the hostile nations whom we find constantly contending with the Egyptians upon their north-eastern frontier."[1] They doubtless claimed the Sinai region as their own and resented any intrusion upon its pasturelands and watering places. The very presence of Israel in the territory aroused their hatred and led to their attack. Apparently at the time they had been pasturing their flocks in the northern regions, nearer Canaan.

The circumstances reveal the vicious nature of the attack. It was *unprovoked.* "Then came Amalek" (v. 8) indicates that they went out of their way to attack Israel. They viewed the Israelites as hostile invaders who must be expelled. Their attack was *cunning* and cruel. From Deuteronomuy 25:17-18 we learn that Amalek came upon Israel and smote the weak and straggling in the rear as Israel was traveling. Moses was in the lead and apparently was not aware of what was taking place until after it had happened. Thus the attack was *unexpected*. After their initial attack the Amalekites encamped in the neighborhood with the intention of renewing the attack the next day.

The attack by Amalek was a distressing experience for Israel. Yet it had a definite value for Israel. It marked the beginning of that process of training whereby Israel was transformed from a motley congregation of ex-slaves into a formidable fighting force. "Just as a mother reaches her hand to a tottering infant, that presently the boy may go alone, so the Lord fought for Israel, that Israel might come to fight for the Lord."[2] God uses the afflictions of His people to develop their spiritual maturity and strength (Rom. 5:3-5; James 1:2-4).

In seeking the symbolic import of this event, some scholars view Amalek as a type of "the flesh," the old unregenerated nature in the believer.[3] But since the conflict is with an external foe, others view the enemy more generally and hold that the attack makes Amalek "the representative of all hostile heathendom, as opposed to the people and kingdom of God."[4] Then this vicious attack by Amalek may be thought of as representative of the Satan-inspired persecution of God's people by the world.

Israel, delivered from bondage, soon encountered this hostility, and believers today likewise do not escape it. Such experiences are never pleasant; yet the Bible has warned us to expect them (cf. John 16:33; Acts 14:22). However, when such opposition does arise many believers are surprised and utterly dismayed. But if our lives reveal the power of God and impinge upon the sphere of the world, we can expect to encounter its hostility.

As we view the world scene we are made keenly aware of the fact that opposition to and persecution of the saints is again a stark reality. It demonstrates that the Church is a power for God which Satan cannot afford to ignore.

A Christian worker connected with an African missionary society once testified that if someone sent him on a journey and told him the road to take, warning him that at a certain point he would come to a dangerous crossing of a river, and at another point he would come to a forest infested with wild beasts, when in his journey he came to that crossing and that forest, then he would know for sure that he was on the right road. So, he remarked, Jesus has sent us on a journey and warned us that Christians will have tribulation and when tribulation comes they know that they are "on the right road." Do we have the evidence that we are on the right road, following Christ's instructions, from the fact that the world opposes and hates us? If we are not encountering any opposition from the world, does not that mean that our lives are so powerless and ineffective that they do not arouse the antagonism of the world?

God is never unaware of or indifferent to such attacks upon His people. In I Samuel 15:2 God says to Samuel, "I remember that which Amalek did to Israel, how he laid wait for him in the way, when he came up from Egypt." God ordered the annihilation of Amalek for his sin (Deut. 25:19; I Sam. 15:3), a punishment accomplished in part by Saul and David (I Sam. 14:48; 15:7; II Sam. 8:12) and completed during the reign of Hezekiah (I Chron. 4:43). The punishment of those who afflict believers may be long delayed, but at last due punishment will be meted out.

II. *The Response of Israel* (vv. 9-10)

1. *The Plan of Moses.* The attack by Amalek doubtless came as an unpleasant surprise to Moses as he was leading his people. But there was no thought of surrender or compromise with the enemy. Courageously he formulated a plan of action to meet the attack. God desires His people to meet such attacks with courage and deliberation. Paul encouraged the afflicted Philippian believers with the assurance, "Your fearlessness will be to them a sure token of impending destruction, but to you it will be a sure token of your salvation" (Phil. 1:28 Weymouth translation).[5]

Moses prudently formulated a plan of action to meet the enemy. The news of the crafty attack on the rear of Israel apparently reached Moses too late for him to take the initiative against the Amalekites that day, but he made plans for appropriate action the next morning. Calling Joshua, he commissioned him to select men and to lead them in battle against the enemy. While Joshua led his men in battle, Moses would stand on the top of the hill with the rod of God in his hand.

2. *The twofold activity.* In repelling the enemy the next day, the Israelites engaged in a double activity. Joshua and his men confronted the enemy in fierce conflict down on the plain while Moses was on the hill holding up the rod of God. This twofold

activity reveals the wisdom and insight of Moses, and the strategy employed also reveals the true secret of success for God's embattled people today.

When the forces of evil are hurling themselves against the Church with deadly intent, a competent leader to direct the activity of the Church in openly repelling the enemy is of vital importance. Effective leaders in the Church in such hours of crisis are of inestimable value. We must appreciate and thank God for all the true and faithful leaders He has given to the churches. They are a gift from the Lord and should be valued and respected as such. Yet these captains over the Lord's warriors must never forget that the victories won are never ultimately due to their own dedicated skill and courage.

Of vital importance is another aspect of the activity going on–Moses on top of the hill with the rod of God in his hand. This part does not seem so spectacular as the other, and the Amalekites doubtless were hardly aware of it and totally ignorant of its crucial significance. Indeed, in all probability most of the Israelites who remained in camp initially never realized the true importance of the activity up on the hill. Wise is that church that recognizes the need for and provides for the employment of both phases of this activity in its warfare against evil.

III. *The Intercession of Moses* (vv. 11-12)

1. *The secret victory* (v. 11). Both activities were essential, but the account reveals that the secret of success in the struggle lay with Moses on the hilltop. When Moses held up his hand with the rod of God, Israel prevailed; but when his hand dropped, Amalek prevailed.

It has been the almost unanimous understanding of commentators, both ancient and modern, that the act of Moses was an act of prayer. It is true that no mention of prayer is made in the account, but the holding up of the rod seems clearly to be a visible appeal to God for further victory by His hand. The holding up of the rod, which God had directed Moses to use in such a marvelous way in the deliverance of Israel, was a confession of dependence on God's power for victory. Although some have understood the holding up of that rod simply as an expression of confidence in Jehovah's power, there is no reason to deny that the lifting up of the rod was also accompanied by fervent prayer for God's help in the conflict.

As long as the hand of Moses was upraised, Israel prevailed because God gave Israel's warriors strength and courage for the battle. The account does not imply that it was simply the sight of that raised hand on the hill that inspired Joshua and his men to fight victoriously. Clearly the power of God was involved. The dropping of the symbol of intercession doubtless also marked the cessation of the supplication. "Probably Moses' spiritual and physical powers collapsed together; and when he dropped his hand through physical fatigue, he rested also from his mental effort."[6]

The strenuous activity on the plain was ineffective without the intercession on the hill. The real secret of success lay not with Joshua but with Moses. The scene thus reveals that intercession is indispensable if the Church is to be victorious. Prayer is a vital means of working for God; *prayer is where the action is.* This "places the intercessor as truly at the front line of spiritual conflict and conquests as the pastor, evangelist, missionary, or any other soldier of the cross. Moreover, the weapons available to him are as effective as those available to the most potent spiritual leader."[7]

Some rather contemptuously contrast the "pray-ers" with the "doers," but they forget that in the history of the Church it has always been the "pray-ers" who have been the effective "doers." The early Church was so dynamic because it was continually in the place of prayer. The widespread activities of Paul were empowered by intensive prayer, his own as well as those of many others. History confirms that men such as Luther, Knox, Wesley, Torrey, and others, who labored mightily for God were themselves mighty men of prayer and had many praying for them.

Prayer is the greatest working power available to the Church today; yet it is the power that is least used. Prayerlessness is the great sin of the Church. Dr. Torrey has well said:

> It was a master stroke of the Devil when he got the church and the ministry so generally to lay aside the mighty weapon of prayer. The Devil is perfectly willing that the church should multiply its organizations and its deftly-contrived machinery for the conquest of the world for Christ, if it will only give up praying. . . . The Devil is not afraid of machinery; he is only afraid of God, and a machinery without prayer is machinery without God.[8]

When we are too busy to pray, we are too busy to have true spiritual power.

In a certain ministers' meeting the chairman asked, "Will every one who spends half an hour every day with God in connection with his work, hold up a hand?" One hand went up. He made a further request: "All those who spend fifteen minutes, hold up a hand." Not half of those present held up a hand. Then he said, "Prayer, the working power of the Church of Christ, and half of the workers hardly make any use of it! All who spend five minutes hold up a hand." All hands went up. But one man came later with the confession that he was not quite sure if he spent five minutes in prayer every day.

2. *The difficulty of perseverance* (vv. 11b-12a). The words "But Moses' hands were heavy" are an acknowledgment of human weakness. They reveal the difficulty of perseverance in prayer. Those who have sought to enter into this ministry of intercession readily confess that they find it much easier to preach an hour than really to pray an hour. But the demand upon Moses for intercession extended vastly beyond an hour!

The weakness of Moses and his need for assistants make it difficult to think of him here as a type of Christ as our intercessor. He is instead a challenging representative of believers in their prayer ministry. The hilltop scene is a picture of saints at prayer, claiming the divine provision for power (the rod of God), yet deeply conscious of their own weakness. Mortal man finds perseverance in intercession a difficult activity. Our efforts to engage actively in this ministry soon lay bare our innate weakness and make us conscious of our human limitations.

3. *The supports for intercession* (v. 12a). The need of Moses for support in his crucial ministry of intercession soon became obvious. His need was met in a very practical way. Moses was seated on a stone while Aaron and Hur stayed his faltering hands and held them steady. The fact that Moses had taken these two leading men with him is evidence of his clear understanding of his own function and his personal limitations in relation to this event. The account of this hilltop scene offers encouraging lessons for us today.

Aaron is the type of Christ our High Priest praying for us and supporting our own faltering intercession. As Aaron supported the weary hand of Moses, so Christ our High Priest supports the intercession of those who have gathered in His name (Matt. 18:19-20). It is most encouraging to recall that we have the support of

Christ before the Father as we present our petitions in His name and plead for victory for His cause.

Moses also received invaluable support from the steadying presence of Hur. If we would know the support of Christ in our intercession we must also know that for which Hur stands. The meaning of his name is not certain but it probably means "whiteness" or "purity." It thus "suggests that purity of heart out of which alone there can be a true calling on the Lord–that purity in the affections which thinks only of the Lord's Name and of what is due to Him."[9] Impurity of life hinders the power of intercession. We cannot forget the injunction that in their prayers men must lift up "holy hands, without wrath and doubting" (I Tim. 2:8).

4. *The duration of the intercession* (v. 12b). "And his hands were steady until the going down of the sun." The fact that the victory was not won until the close of the day eloquently testifies to the strength and determination of the enemy. We too face a mighty foe who has waged relentless war against the people of God down through the centuries.

Joshua and his soldiers fought hard on the plain, but how important for their success was the fact that those hands remained uplifted on the hilltop. We thank God for all our brave Christian warriors who are openly meeting the enemy in spiritual conflict; but how they need the empowerment of our prayers. Their own prayers and activities are charged with power as prayer is continually being made for them in the churches. The greatest service which we can render God's warriors on the field of battle is to intercede for them.

A veteran missionary had just reported to his home church concerning the needs on the field. After the service a young man approached him, expressed his appreciation for the report, and commented, "We will be sending you something more important than our prayers." "You cannot do that," the missionary instantly replied; "prayer is the most important support that you can send us." Missionaries have always recognized the importance of intercessory support and earnestly plead for it.

Because you prayed–
God touched our lips with coals from altar fire,
Gave Spirit-fulness, and did so inspire
That, when we spoke, sin-blinded souls did see;
Sin's chains were broken; captives were made free.

Because you prayed—
The dwellers in the dark have found the Light;
The glad good news has banished heathen night;
The message of the cross, so long delayed,
Has brought them life at last—because you prayed.

—Charles B. Bowser

IV. *The Outcome of the Intercession* (vv. 13-16)

1. *The victory over Amalek* (v. 13). The ultimate victory of Israel over the aggressive Amalekites was intimately related to the intercession of Moses. Those uplifted hands assured decisive victory in the end. Joshua ''discomfited''—more literally ''prostrated''—the attacking enemy, overwhelming him in conscious defeat. The power of Amalek and those associated with him was effectively broken.

In our conflict with the opposing forces of the world, sin, and Satan, we too have the assurance that ours is a victorious cause. The battle may sway to and fro during the conflict of the day, but the final victory of God's cause is assured. We have the Lord's assurance: ''In the world ye shall have tribulation: but be of good cheer; I have overcome the world'' (John 16:33).

2. *The instruction of Israel* (v. 14). Following the victory over Amalek, the Lord instructed Moses to record an account of the attack and to preserve it in living memory. There could never be peace and friendship between Israel and Amalek. So too, believers must ever remember that as the people of God they can never enter into a covenant of friendship with a Christ-rejecting world (James 4:4).

God further informed Moses that Amalek, as the enemy of God's chosen people, would certainly be destroyed. God assured Moses, ''I will utterly put out the remembrance of Amalek from under heaven.'' This prophecy of the extermination of Amalek was later fulfilled through God's orders to the kings of Israel. Although God's people may suffer unjustly from the attacks of the enemy, in the end God will vindicate them and mete out justice to all.

3. *The altar of worship* (vv. 15-16). The altar unto the Lord which Moses built implies that he offered thank-offerings in acknowledgment of the signal victory which God had given. God's marvelous working in answer to prayer can fill the heart

of His saints only with joy and thanksgiving for His wonderful deeds. They readily join with the psalmist in saying, "Oh that men would praise the Lord for his goodness, and for his wonderful works to the children of men!" (Ps. 107:8).

The altar also served as a memorial, a monument proclaiming that the true victor was Jehovah. Moses called the altar "Jehovah-nissi," which means "Jehovah is my banner." The altar would bear witness to all who heard its name that at that site a battle had taken place and that the victory belonged to the people who had made Jehovah their God. God Himself was their banner, and the true source of the victory was not the rod held up on the hilltop but the God to whom Moses made his persevering appeal. The name of the altar "is a declaration of faith in the reality of divine help, so real and so convincing that they will never again dissociate themselves from Him."[10]

Moses explained why God had given such a great victory. The Hebrew of verse 16 may quite literally be rendered "Because his hand [i.e., Amalek's] is on the throne of Jehovah, (there shall be) war to Jehovah with Amalek from generation to generation." By his vicious attack upon Israel, Amalek had lifted up his hand against the throne of Jehovah; therefore, God Himself would fight against Amalek. Those who are assured that the cause for which they are interceding is God's work can persevere because they know that in His time God will give the victory. "Thanks be to God, which giveth us the victory through our Lord Jesus Christ." (I Cor. 15:57).

Notes

[1]George Rawlinson, "The Second Book of Moses, Called Exodus," in *Ellicott's Commentary on the Whole Bible* (Reprint ed., Grand Rapids: Zondervan, n.d.), 1:251.

[2]G. A. Chadwick, "The Book of Exodus," in *An Exposition of the Bible* (Hartford, Conn.: The S. S. Scranton Co., 1903), 1:184.

[3]Arno C. Gaebelein, *The Annotated Bible* (Reprint ed., Chicago: Moody Press, 1970), 1:149; C. I. Scofield, ed., *The Scofield Reference Bible* (1917), p. 91, note 3. *The New Scofield Reference Bible* (1967) omits the note.

[4]John Peter Lange, "Exodus," in *Lange's Commentary on the Holy Scriptures,* vol. 2, *Exodus-Leviticus* (1876; reprint ed., Grand Rapids: Zondervan, n.d.), p. 66.

[5]Richard Francis Weymouth, *The New Testament in Modern Speech,* 5th ed. (New York: Harper and Brothers, 1929).

[6]George Rawlinson, ''The Book of Exodus,'' in *The Pulpit Commentary* (Reprint ed., Chicago: Wilcox and Follett Co., n.d.), 2:72.

[7]Paul E. Billheimer, *Destined for the Throne* (Fort Washington, Pa.: Christian Literature Crusade, 1975), pp. 103-4.

[8]R. A. Torrey, *How to Obtain Fullness of Power in Christian Life and Service* (1897; reprint ed., Wheaton, Ill.: Sword of the Lord Publishers, n.d.), p. 59.

[9]C. A. Coates, *An Outline of the Book of Exodus* (Kingston-on-Thames, England: Stow Hill Bible and Tract Society, n.d.), p. 100.

[10]John Macbeath, *What Is His Name?* (London: Marshall, Morgan & Scott, n.d.), p. 56.

VI

The Prayer of Jabez

And Jabez was more honourable than his brethren: and his mother called his name Jabez, saying, Because I bare him with sorrow. And Jabez called on the God of Israel, saying, Oh that thou wouldest bless me indeed, and enlarge my coast, and that thine hand might be with me, and that thou wouldest keep me from evil, that it may not grieve me! And God granted him that which he requested. (I Chron. 4:9-10)

These beautiful verses tell the story of a man who knew the secret of working by prayer. They draw us like a refreshing oasis in the midst of a desert of strange and unpronounceable names. This spiritual gem is a rich reward for faithfulness in reading through these chapters of unfamiliar names.

All that the Bible tells us about this Old Testament man of prayer is contained in this biographical note. God has a way at times of writing the biography of His saints in brief; yet these concise biographies are luminous with spiritual truth. This biography of Jabez memorializes him as a man of prayer, a man who labored for God through prayer. Could the Holy Spirit thus summarize our life?

Three features arrest attention as we study this account of Jabez, the man of prayer: the man who prayed, the prayer he prayed, and the answer he received.

I. *The Man Who Prayed* (v. 9)

It is always interesting to know about a man who prays; a man's character has much to do with his praying. It largely determines the kind of prayer he can offer and the answer he receives. Verse 9 records two matters concerning the history of Jabez: his achievement of outstanding honor and the ominous name given him by his mother. The very order of these two facts seems to suggest a feeling of triumph in the preservation of his story. His achievement was noteworthy in the light of his adverse background.

1. *Adverse background.* The comment of Jabez's mother in naming her son clearly indicated the unfavorable background which he overcame. In giving her infant the ominous name "Jabez," which means "causing pain or sorrow," the mother's explanatory comment is, "Because I bare him with sorrow." Just what caused her somber reaction is not known. It may have been some physical deformity or some other obvious difficulty which indicated to her that the child would face personal handicap in life. Others, such as White, surmise that the name was due to the tragic circumstances of the family at the time of the child's birth.[1] Whatever the cause of her grief, her gloomy reaction in giving him this name destined the boy throughout his life to be the symbol of her sorrow.

The story of Jabez is suddenly introduced in these genealogical chapters without any indication of his precise family connections. It has been suggested that his name is a corruption of, or second name for, one of the names mentioned in the preceding verse. (It has been held, for instance, that his name is a corruption of Zobebah in verse 8.[2] Keil notes that the older commentators concluded that Jabez was a son or brother of Coz in verse 8.[3] Neither suggestion is capable of proof.) The indirect reference to his brothers indicates that there was a family circle; the fact that the author does not name "his brethren" may suggest that he deemed them unworthy of being named along with Jabez. Fairbairn thinks that the account suggests that the life of Jabez was also "peculiarly associated with experiences of trouble" since the recorded prayer of Jabez implies that he cried to God amid personal distress.[4] In his own experience Jabez obviously did not wholly escape the implications of his name.

2. *Outstanding honor.* In spite of his unfavorable background, Jabez made good in life. This brief biography memorializes him as a man who achieved outstanding honor.

Early Jewish writers connected Jabez with the town of that name mentioned in I Chronicles 2:55 and concluded that he was an eminent doctor in the law.[5] They held that his learning drew so many scholars around him that the place where they resided came to be called by his name. This conjecture would certainly enhance the honor of Jabez, but this proposed connection between the man and the town cannot be verified.

The Biblical account connects the eminence of Jabez with the fact that he was a man of prayer. He excelled his brothers in the realm of fellowship with God, resulting in his excellence of character. Whether or not his brothers excelled in other areas of life, Jabez stood unquestionably first as a man of piety.

Here is a field of endeavor that is open to everyone regardless of the limitations or unfavorable circumstances under which he may live. Jabez did not allow the implications of his name to make him feel that he was doomed to failure. His achievement is a challenge to all who feel that they are severely restricted by an unfortunate environment or inevitably defeated by a personal handicap.

The secret of the success of Jabez lies in his prayer life. It is upon his prayer that the Biblical record lays special emphasis.

II. *The Prayer He Prayed* (v. 10a)

More space is given to the prayer of Jabez than to his achievement of outstanding honor. "His prayer," says Fausset," is one of the most comprehensive in the Bible, and shines forth like a brilliant star in the midst of a genealogical catalogue of names."[6] It was his praying that made the man so outstanding.

1. *To whom he prayed.* "And Jabez called on the God of Israel." One can view the expression "the God of Israel" in two different ways. The reference may be to the man Jacob who became Israel. Jabez well knew the story of Jacob and how God had changed him from a deceiver into a saint and may well have believed that if God could do that for a Jacob, surely He could also help him. And the God who transformed Jacob into Israel is still able to change the lives of those who will give Him an opportunity to do so. Have we given the God of Jacob an opportunity to show what He can do with us?

It is more probable, however, that in calling upon "the God of Israel," Jabez thought of Him as the God of the nation of Israel. He himself was a member of that nation. He had ample reasons to call upon his God with confidence and assurance.

Jabez knew what God had done for the nation of Israel, how He had marvelously redeemed it, led it, supplied its every need, and protected it from its enemies. He had answered the prayers of Moses on behalf of the people in spite of their sin and rebellion. Jabez could remember the mighty revelations which God had given His people. Not only had He given them His law, but also He had shown Himself as their redeemer, leader, provider, healer, and protector; He was a God concerned about the needs of His people. Such a God Jabez knew he could approach with complete confidence.

But Jabez also knew that "the God of Israel" had entered into covenant relations with Israel. Jehovah had selected the Israelites as His chosen people and had given them wondrous revelations and high privileges. Being a member of that covenant nation, Jabez could call upon "the God of Israel" in full assurance of faith that he would receive an audience with God. And we too, who have been brought near to God through the New Covenant established in Christ Jesus, can call upon Him in full assurance of access to Him.

2. *How he prayed.* In the Hebrew the prayer of Jabez is expressed in the form of an unfinished vow to God. "If thou wilt bless me indeed and enlarge my coast, and thine hand will be with me, and thou wilt keep me from evil, that it may not grieve me. . . ." The sentence remains unfinished. Of his prayer-vow, only the conditions proposed by Jabez are uttered, while that which he intended to vow to God remains unstated. The form implies that Jabez uttered his prayer-vow as he was about to enter upon some important or critical activity. Perhaps, as Jamieson suggests, the occasion was when Jabez undertook to expel the Canaanites from the territory which had been allotted to his family.[7] Instead of his vow, the record states the divine fulfilment of his conditional desires. The implication is that God, who knew the heartfelt desires and motives of Jabez before he expressed them, readily granted his request. It was a prayer in accord with God's will for Jabez. First John 3:21-22 assures us that such prayer receives an answer from God.

3. *What he prayed.* Jabez was explicit in his requests. He gave expression in his prayer to four distinct petitions, constituting a logical progression of thought.

a. For a *divine blessing*. "Oh that thou wouldest bless me indeed." Jabez considered the divine blessing of primary importance and made it his first request. He knew that without God's blessing all other things are of but little value. Do we?

Jabez realized that all true blessings come from God: "Oh that *thou* wouldest bless me." He knew that it was Jehovah God who had blessed the nation of Israel, and he eagerly desired the same God to bless him personally. Jabez thus laid hold on a truth that many of his fellow Israelites forgot when they forsook the true God and turned to the idols of the nations around them. May the precious truth that "the God and Father of our Lord Jesus Christ . . . hath blessed us with all spiritual blessings in heavenly places in Christ" (Eph. 1:3) ever be a vital reality to us.

Jabez ardently desired a definite personal blessing from his God. "Bless me *indeed*" carries an intensive force in the original, "surely or richly bless." It is the language of ardent and affectionate desire. He was not content with a vague feeling of general well-being but wanted to experience the divine blessing in a definite, personal way. If the blessings of God are to be real and vital to us, they must be appropriated and experienced individually.

b. For *divine enlargement*. In praying "and enlarge my coast," or "border," Jabez was praying for more land to possess, more real estate. That sounds very modern, does it not? The request has indeed been stamped as "crude and selfish."[8] But before we condemn Jabez for his request, let us consider the background for this petition. The setting may be viewed in one of two different ways.

Jabez may be thought of as preparing to wrest more of the Promised Land from the Canaanites. God had promised the land of Canaan to Abraham, Isaac, and Jacob. God renewed that promise to the nation of Israel through Joshua just before it crossed the river Jordan (Josh. 1:2-4). Israel had entered the land but had conquered only part of it. The Lord reminded Joshua shortly before his death that "there remaineth yet very much land to be possessed" (Josh. 13:1). Thus Jabez may be pictured as asking God to give him more of that which He had promised to His people. It took faith to believe that God would give him the land when it was still in the possession of the enemy. And so in faith Jabez made a worthy request for more of the very thing which God had promised to His people. Or Jabez may be viewed as asking God to enable him to restore the fortunes of his family in Israel as he seeks to repossess all of the land given to his family by divine allotment.[9] Then he is to be thought of as seeking to repair the failures of the past within the family circle and to renew the hopes of the rising generation for the future.

Under either view Jabez cannot be charged with selfishness in asking for divine enlargement. He rightly desired to possess more of that which God had intended for His people to have. He could freely make this request because his first desire was to be personally worthy of God's blessing. It was an attitude that spiritually qualified him to be entrusted with more of the things of God.

When William E. Blackstone was a man in the prime of his life he exclaimed, "Oh that God would give me a million dollars! I would use every penny for the evangelization of the world!" The Lord knew that by training and experience he was competent to administer such enormous funds; He also knew that Blackstone could be entrusted with such wealth. The Lord, therefore, providentially placed in his hands five million dollars for evangelization purposes. He was faithful as a trustee of this fund, and myriads of souls came to know the Lord because W. E. Blackstone prayed, as did Jabez of old, "Enlarge my border."[10]

c. For *divine strengthening*. "And that thine hand might be with me." The "hand of God" here denotes His guiding presence and His empowerment. Jabez surely felt a need for the guiding hand of God in his undertaking. He knew that God must lead him, but he also realized his need of the manifestation of God's power in his behalf. Jabez would readily have joined the psalmist in praying, "Let thine hand help me; for I have chosen thy precepts" (Ps. 119:173).

His petition was a confession of his own weakness. When he looked at himself he felt as helpless to achieve his goal as did the ten spies, but unlike the ten spies he had the faith of Joshua and Caleb which looked to God for the needed empowerment.

When St. Theresa was laughed at because she wanted to build an orphanage and had but three shillings to begin with, she answered, "With three shillings Theresa can do nothing; but with God and three shillings there is nothing that Theresa cannot do." Blessed is that believer who has experienced his own inability to do Christian work in his own strength and has learned to cast himself unreservedly upon the power of God to perform all such service. The secret of the empowered life is to be found in continued "abiding" in Christ. "He that abideth in me, and I in him, the same bringeth forth much fruit: for without me ye can do nothing" (John 15:5).

d. For *divine protection.* "And that thou wouldest keep me from evil, that it may not grieve me." Jabez further asked that, in his struggle to attain the enlarged purposes of God for him, God would so work that "evil," or harm, would be kept away. He asked to be kept from evil because he knew and feared its sorrowful consequences. He desired that the ominous implications of his name might not be repeated in his own experiences. He had but to recall his mother's feelings to be assured that evil always results in grief and sorrow.

Jabez realized that left to himself he would inevitably succumb to the power of evil. He confessed a need for restraining power against evil stronger than his own power. He found that power in God. It is this truth experientially realized that leads the believer to cast himself fully upon his God for protection from evil and for empowerment to meet the trials of life. This is the road to spiritual victory.

The order of the petitions of Jabez shows a logical progression. He began his prayer by acknowledging the blessings of God as his highest good. This step led to a desire for a larger share in the riches which God has prepared for His people. In his efforts to attain these blessings he realized his own weakness and pleaded for divine guidance and empowerment for victory. And in his struggles he came to see himself aright and was led to throw himself unreservedly upon the grace of God. And it was there that he found the desired blessings and victory.

III. *The Answer He Received* (v. 10b)

The ultimate test of every prayer is the answer that it receives. The answer proves the acceptableness of the prayer, and the prayer of Jabez triumphantly passed this test.

1. *Answer received.* "And God granted," more literally, "And God brought about." The fulfillment of his desires was not due to fortuitous circumstances. The God of Jabez was at work in shaping the outcome. His experience confirmed that prayer out of a true heart and according to His will receives God's answer.

I know not by what methods rare,
But this I know, God answers prayer;
I know that He has giv'n His word
Which tells me prayer is always heard,
And will be answered, soon or late;
And so I pray, and calmly wait.

I know not if the blessing sought
Will come in just the way I thought;
But leave my prayers with Him alone,
Whose will is wiser than my own,
Assured that He will grant my quest,
Or send some answer far more blest.

–Eliza M. Hickok

2. *Exact answer.* "And God granted him *that which* he requested." Jabez received what he asked for. This answer is evidence that his prayer was in the will of God for him. "We have this assurance in approaching God, that if we ask anything according to his will, he hears us. And if we know that he hears us–whatever we ask–we know that we have what we asked of him" (I John 5:14-15 NIV).

The prayer of Jabez, because it was in accordance with God's will, furthered Jehovah's intention for His people, Israel. This prayer of faith, desiring only God's will and the honor of His name, is always a mighty power for the advancement of the kingdom of God.

Notes

[1]Reginald E. O. White, *They Teach Us to Pray. A Biographical ABC of the Prayer Life* (New York: Harper & Brothers, 1957), pp. 53-54.

[2]Edward Lewis Curtis and Albert Alonzo Madsen, *A Critical and Exegetical Commentary on the Books of Chronicles,* The International Critical Commentary (New York: Charles Scribner's Sons, 1910), p. 107.

[3]C. F. Keil, *The Books of the Chronicles,* Biblical Commentary on the Old Testament, trans. Andrew Harper (Reprint ed., Grand Rapids: Eerdmans, 1950), p. 88.

[4]Patrick Fairbairn, *Imperial Standard Bible Encyclopedia* (1891; reprint ed., Grand Rapids: Zondervan, 1957), 3:184.

[5]Robert Jamieson and A. R. Fausset, *A Commentary, Critical and Explanatory, on the Old Testament,* vol. 1, *Old Testament* (Hartford, Conn.: The S. S. Scranton Co., n.d.), p. 251.

[6]A. R. Fausset, *Bible Cyclopaedia, Critical and Explanatory* (Hartford, Conn.: The S. S. Scranton Co., 1902), p. 321.

[7]Jamieson and Fausett, p. 251.

[8]W.A.L. Elmslie, ''The First and Second Books of Chronicles,'' in *The Interpreter's Bible* (New York: Abingdon, 1954), 3:359.

[9]White, p. 57.

[10]David L. Cooper, ''The Prayer of Jabez,'' *Biblical Research Monthly,* vol. 9, no. 1 (1944), p. 4.

VII

Epaphras, Man of Prayer

Epaphras, who is one of you, a servant of Christ Jesus, saluteth you, always striving for you in his prayers, that ye may stand perfect and fully assured in all the will of God. For I bear him witness, that he hath much labor for you, and for them in Laodicea, and for them in Hierapolis. (Col. 4:12-13 ASV)

As an intimate friend of the Apostle Paul, Epaphras had grasped the tremendous possibilities of working by prayer. So aggressively had he taken up this ministry while with Paul at Rome that even Paul, the apostle of prayer, was impressed. Epaphras holds the unique distinction among all the friends and co-workers of Paul of being the only one whom Paul explicitly commended for his intensive prayer ministry. The passage quoted above may well be called his diploma of success in this ministry.

All that we know about this man Epaphras must be gleaned from the few references to him contained in the apostle's twin letters, Colossians and Philemon, sent to the city of Colossae by the hand of Tychicus. Epaphras's name occurs only three times in these two letters (Col. 1:7; 4:12; Philem. 23), and only five verses in all refer to him. Yet these brief glimpses of Epaphras afford us an attractive picture of this prayer warrior whose highest distinction lay in the record of his intense prayer labors. His Christian character and his deep pastoral concerns eminently qualified him for this ministry.

The name Epaphras is apparently a shortened form of the common name Epaphroditus, which means handsome or charming. In the letter to the Philippians, Epaphroditus appears as the representative of the Philippian church who brought an offering to Paul in Rome. But the two men are not to be confused.

I. *The Characterization of Epaphras* (v. 12a)

In Colossians 1:7 Paul has already named Epaphras as the one through whom the Colossians first heard the gospel. But in closing his letter, Paul once more adds a significant characterization of this man.

1. *Connection with Colossae.* Paul begins by identifying Epaphras as "one of you." The reference would at once stir the interest of the Colossian Christians. The expression, also used of Onesimus in verse 9 above, indicates that Epaphras was a native, or at least a permanent resident, of Colossae.

Paul did not personally found the church at Colossae (Col. 2:1), but its origin appears to be directly related to the time of his three-year ministry at Ephesus during the third missionary journey. During those busy, fruitful years at Ephesus, the gospel was widely disseminated throughout the province of Asia, as Luke testifies (Acts 19:10). As the metropolis of Asia, Ephesus drew throngs of visitors from all parts of the province, coming for business, pleasure, or worship. While in Ephesus many of these visitors came into contact with the gospel, were converted, and carried the Good News back to their homes.

It would appear that Epaphras, while on a visit to Ephesus, came into personal contact with the Apostle Paul, heard the glorious message of salvation, and accepted Christ as his own Saviour. Epaphras revealed himself as an eager and apt pupil of Paul and won the apostle's love and esteem. Epaphras soon felt that he must return home to share the wonderful message of salvation in Christ with his neighbors and friends. He soon found himself back among his old acquaintances but with the new message of salvation on his lips.

From Colossians 1:7 it is clear that the gospel was first brought to Colossae by Epaphras: "even as ye learned of Epaphras" (ASV).[1] Epaphras did not merely confirm the message they already knew; he was the messenger from whom they originally heard the Good News. The better attested reading, designating Epaphras as "a faithful minister of Christ *on our behalf*" (ASV), indicates that it was as Paul's representative that he worked at Colossae. Since Paul felt that he could not leave his important and fruitful work at Ephesus, he gladly commissioned Epaphras to go back with the gospel as his approved representative. The work of Epaphras resulted in the formation of the Colossian church, and perhaps the churches in Laodicea and Hierapolis (4:13).

Apparently Epaphras continued on as the shepherd of the flock at Colossae. He thus stood in an intimate relationship with the believers at Colossae as the founder and spiritual teacher of the church there. As "one of you," Epaphras was just an ordinary individual but one upon whom God had laid His hand for use as His agent to bring the gospel to his own people.

2. *Relation to Christ.* Epaphras stood in an intimately spiritual relationship with his Lord. It is noteworthy that in all three places where his name occurs, it appears in direct connection with that of Christ. In 1:7 he is commended as "a faithful minister of Christ," while here he is termed "a servant of Christ Jesus" (ASV). The designations are high tribute to Epaphras. Paul several times uses the latter designation of himself. It is once used of Timothy in conjunction with the apostle's name (Phil. 1:1). Epaphras is the only other individual to whom the title is applied. It points to exceptional service in the cause of Christ on the part of Epaphras.

The word rendered "servant" is the ordinary Greek term for a slave. However, in such connections the emphasis is not upon the compulsory service of the slave but rather upon the intimate relationship of the servant with his master. Hendriksen thus summarizes the rich implications of this designation: "A servant of Christ Jesus is one who has been bought with a price and is therefore owned by his Master, on whom he is completely dependent, to whom he owes undivided allegiance and to whom he ministers with gladness of heart, in newness of spirit, and in the enjoyment of perfect freedom, receiving from him a glorious reward!"[2] The term proclaims the servant's unconditional surrender of himself to do his Lord's bidding. Such a one has learned to say,

Oh, teach my will, my selfish will,
    To be completely Thine.
Oh, may I yield my all to Thee;
    It is no longer mine.

Oh, may my will, my stubborn will,
    Submissive be to Thine;
The inward man obey with joy
    The law of love divine.

Anyone who has not yet come to the place of full yieldedness of himself to his Lord will never know the joy of fruitful service and effective intercession that Epaphras attained. The yielded will lies at the basis of the God-used life.

3. *Greetings to Colossians.* Being with Paul as the apostle was concluding the letter to the Colossians, Epaphras expressed his desire that his affectionate greetings to the believers at home be included. Paul gladly included the greetings from Epaphras and used the occasion to give the Colossians further information about Epaphras. Although separated from them, his love and deep pastoral concern did not allow Epaphras to be unmindful of them. And it was his very concern for the Colossian believers that explains his presence with Paul at Rome.

Some five years or so had passed since the founding of the Colossian church. Paul was now a prisoner in Rome, and Epaphras had gone there to confer with Paul. Recently an insidious new teaching had begun to manifest itself in Colossae, a subtle and alluring doctrine that threatened to make havoc of the work for Christ that had been accomplished. The new teaching claimed to be Christian but was undermining the gospel by robbing Christ of His unique nature and authority. Epaphras felt himself unable to refute this heresy effectively. Acting upon a strong desire to present the matter to the Apostle Paul, Epaphras had made the long journey to Rome to get Paul's help.

In making his report to Paul, Epaphras had given a favorable account of the general condition of the church (1:8; 2:5). But his faithful report also contained information about the new teaching at Colossae, which filled the mind of Paul with deep anxiety for them (2:1-4), an anxiety which Epaphras fully shared with him. Having informed himself concerning the true nature of this new doctrine as described to him by Epaphras, and having given himself to earnest prayer and thought about it (1:9; 2:1-3), Paul dealt with the situation in the letter now being dispatched to the Colossians. The letter was the fruit of the pastoral concern of Epaphras for his people.

Since the letter was sent to Colossae with Tychicus (4:7-9), it is obvious that Epaphras was not returning immediately. Interpreters have suggested different explanations for his continued stay in Rome. Some think that the stay of Epaphras was not voluntary. In Philemon 23 Paul refers to Epaphras as "my fellowprisoner." This statement has led to the supposition that his close relationship with Paul in Rome had aroused suspicion and had caused his own arrest. Martin even suggests that "this detention from his pastoral responsibility at home filled him with painful anxiety."[3] But this deduction from Paul's designation is questionable. In Colossians 4:10 the designation "my fellowprisoner" is applied to Aristarchus but is withheld from Epaphras, while in Philemon Aristarchus is simply called a "fellow worker." Perhaps the best explanation for this variation in Paul's use of the designation is the view that these two men voluntarily took turns in closely sharing Paul's confinement. Paul thus gave expression to his deep appreciation of their devotion and service to him in those tedious hours.

Having come such a long distance to confer with Paul, Epaphras apparently felt constrained to prolong his close contact with Paul because of the personal enrichment he experienced. It would enable him to serve his people better upon his return. In the meantime, he had not forgotten his flock at home and felt that he could render them an effective service through his prayers for them. "The best scene of memory is at the throne of grace."[4]

II. *The Praying of Epaphras* (v. 12b)

In sending the greetings of Epaphras, Paul thought it important to inform the Colossians of the prayers of Epaphras on their behalf. Although absent from them, Epaphras was thus rendering them a valuable service.

1. *Fact of his praying.* The very fact that Epaphras was praying for his flock while absent from them was an indication of his spiritual character. His prayer concern for them was an indication of the high level of his own inner experience. "Certainly, as water never rises above its level, so our service in its quality, reality, vitality and energy will never be higher than the genuineness of our fellowship with God."[5]

Epaphras was unable to write the letter to the Colossians as Paul did, refuting the heretical teaching which was disturbing them, but he could faithfully pray for their preservation and spiritual maturity. Paul gratefully recorded that Epaphras was engaged in such a prayer ministry for the readers. The example of Epaphras is a challenge to ordinary Christians to engage in this important ministry. Griffith Thomas well says, ''There are many things outside the power of ordinary Christian people, and great position, wide influence, outstanding ability may be lacking to almost all of us, but the humblest and least significant Christian can pray, and as 'prayer moves the Hand that moves the world,' perhaps the greatest power we can exert is that which comes through prayer.''[6]

2. *Nature of his praying.* The apostle describes the praying of Epaphras in the following significant words: ''always striving for you in his prayers'' (ASV). This brief statement is richly instructive.

a. *Constant.* Paul bore witness that Epaphras was ''always striving'' for the Colossian Christians. It was not an occasional, listless prayer on their behalf but a constant burden of intercession. Regularly and repeatedly he bore them up before the throne of grace. His deep concern for them made him obedient to the words of our Lord that ''men ought always to pray, and not to faint'' (Luke 18:1).

b. *Definite.* Paul assured the Colossians that Epaphras was always praying ''for you.'' Their spiritual welfare was his predominant concern, and he kept them prominent in his prayers. His was not that indefinite kind of praying about which one would be hard pressed to tell for whom the petition was intended. He was aware of the danger that threatened them, and he prayed accordingly. His specific petitions revealed that Epaphras had the heart of a true shepherd of God's flock.

In the days when the family pew was an institution of the church, the story is related that every Saturday afternoon neighbors and passers-by would see an old pastor leave his study and enter the church by the back door, remain there for a period of time, and then return home about sundown. One man, his curiosity aroused, followed the pastor one day and watched through a window. The hidden onlooker saw the old pastor kneel at each pew and pray for every member of the family that was to occupy it on the Lord's Day. He called each member by name as he poured out his heart to God for his flock. His was a ministry of power, and his people reflected the grace of God upon them. Blessed is that church which has such a praying shepherd.

c. *Intense.* Significantly Paul describes the praying of Epaphras for his people as "striving" for them (ASV). The verb indicates that it was a strenuous and costly activity. The term comes from the athletic arena and pictures the intense effort and energy of the athlete in contending for a prize, like a wrestler grappling in all earnestness with his opponent. It is the verbal form of the noun *agony* that Luke employs to describe Christ's praying in Gethsemane (Luke 22:44). The term clearly portrays the difficulty of effective intercessory prayer. "True prayer," says Maclaren, "is the intensest energy of the spirit pleading for blessing with a great striving of faithful desire."[7]

We find an illustration of such intense, working prayer in the life of the prophet Daniel, as recorded in the ninth chapter of his book. For three weeks Daniel afflicted himself and wrestled in prayer against the forces of spiritual wickedness until their powers were broken and the answer came. The prayers of Daniel, as undoubtedly also those of Epaphras, were a definite means of advancing the cause of God.

3. *Aim of his praying.* The words "that ye may stand perfect and fully assured in all the will of God" (ASV) indicates not the contents of his prayers but rather his pastoral desire for the Colossians. Epaphras knew the result he expected from his prayers. He had grasped the reality of ministering to his people through his prayers for them. Forbes Robinson of Cambridge remarked that instead of calling on a man or inviting an individual to call him, he found it more profitable to spend a half-hour in concentrated prayer for him. He knew the reality of working by prayer.

a. *Desire for stability.* In praying for the Colossian Christians, Epaphras was well aware of the potentially disastrous results if they were lured away by the heretical teaching at work in the Lycus River Valley. But he was not merely concerned about their preservation from error. His deeper concern was for the positive, balanced development of their Christian character. Spiritual maturity would enable them to stand firm.

The aorist passive form of the verb "may stand" suggests their need of empowerment from without that would enable them to stand, that is, "be made to stand." Such stability would result from the impartation of divine strength through the Holy Spirit. In the face of multiplying heresies, whether subtle or flagrant, it is imperative that believers become firmly rooted and grounded in the truth. The need today is for men like Epaphras, whose persevering prayers are focused upon troubled believers so that they may become firmly established in faith and God-pleasing conduct.

b. *Manifestation of stability*. Epaphras prayed that the stability desired for his people might manifest itself in their lives in Christian maturity and assurance: "That ye may stand perfect and fully assured" (ASV).

The word "perfect" does not imply sinlessness but rather means spiritual maturity. Christians are to become fully grown adults as contrasted to spiritual babes. The believer becomes "perfect" or complete as he attains unto the divine goal for his life. Such maturity of character the believer finds only in abiding union with Christ.

Epaphras further desired that the Colossian believers might stand "fully assured in all the will of God." The tense of the verbal form (a perfect participle) indicates his desire that this may be their abiding condition. The new teaching was harassing their souls and confusing their minds. The concern of Epaphras was that they might be freed from all doubts and uncertainty. The soul that is torn by doubts and uncertainty as to what God's will requires cannot stand firm under testing and trial. Maclaren well says, "To be free from misery of intellectual doubts and practical uncertainties, to walk in the sunshine–is the purest joy."[8]

Epaphras prayed that their stability would manifest itself "in all the will of God." Interpreters have understood the precise connection of this phrase in different ways, but it seems best to take it as modifying the entire purpose clause. It thus indicates that the will of God is to be the governing consideration in their stability. Lightfoot translated the phrase "in everything willed by God."[9] The desire of Epaphras is that under every circumstance they make God's will the object of their attentive consideration and implicit obedience. "All" or "everything" points to the varied circumstances into which the believer is permitted to come and in which he desires to adhere to the divine will. Amid all circumstances may they have an understanding of God's will "which not only penetrates the mind but also fills the heart with satisfying conviction."[10]

III. *The Testimony to Epaphras* (v. 13)

Having described the prayer ministry of Epaphras, Paul confirmed and approved that ministry with his own testimony.

1. *Person giving testimony.* The opening "for" is confirmatory. Paul had himself observed and been deeply impressed with the strenuous prayer labors of Epaphras. Ever since Paul had heard about the condition of affairs at Colossae, he had given himself to a definite ministry of intercession for the saints there (1:9; 2:1). And at Rome Epaphras had fully entered into that prayer struggle. He had shown himself "Paul's true scholar in the school of intercession."[11] The apostle delighted to recognize the prayer labors in which Epaphras was engaged.

2. *Occasion for testimony.* The fact that Paul felt it necessary to add this personal testimony to his vivid account of the praying of Epaphras does not seem to be without significance. It has been pointed out that in other places where Paul uses the expression, "I bear witness," attention is called to something noteworthy under the circumstances. It may well be that, perhaps because of the reaction of the false teachers at Colossae, there had been some opposition to the trip of Epaphras to consult with Paul. Some believers may have felt that under the circumstances it was evident that Epaphras really desired to sever connections with them. Paul had already expressed his full approval of the work of Epaphras at Colossae (1:3-8); the present strenuous prayer labors of Epaphras on their behalf established that his love and concern for them had not diminished.

Apparently Paul also realized that some might question the fact that Epaphras was remaining in Rome rather than returning at once with the letter from Paul. In thus adding his own testimony, Paul would assure them that although Epaphras was absent from them, he had not forgotten them, and his love was expressing itself in a sacrificial ministry of toil in intercession. If the Colossians were like modern Christians, it is quite likely that many of them did not have an adequate appreciation of the value of the service which Epaphras was rendering them. Paul's warm testimony of approval would increase their appreciation of what Epaphras was doing.

3. *Content of testimony.* Paul's testimony touches both the strenuousness and the scope of the prayer labors of Epaphras.

Paul indicates the strenuousness of those prayer labors when he remarks that "he hath *much labor* for you" (ASV).[12] The word rendered "labor" occurs only here in the writings of Paul. It carries the idea of great effort, toil, or strenuous exertion. The view that the reference is to the hard work of Epaphras while still at home, either in seeking to counteract the new teaching[13] or laboring to provide financial help for the people stricken by an earthquake,[14] is inconsistent with Paul's use of the present tense. Paul's term seems best understood as continuing the picture of striving presented in the previous verse; the apostle's words confirm and strengthen the point that the prayers of Epaphras involved intense mental and spiritual effort. In view of his own experience, Paul readily recognized the intensity of those labors.

The scope of the prayer labors of Epaphras is indicated in the words "for you, and for them in Laodicea, and for them in Hierapolis" (ASV). The three cities, located in the Lycus River Valley, are indicated in their geographical order, beginning at Colossae. Colossae, the smallest of the three cities, was the farthest east. Laodicea, the largest and most prosperous of the three cities, was some eleven or twelve miles west, a little south of the Lycus River. About six miles north of Laodicea, across the Lycus, stood the city of Hierapolis. One could easily visit all three cities in one day. The churches in all three cities were obviously confronted with the same heretical teaching.

The fact that Epaphras engaged in prayer for the believers in all three cities shows his personal interest and concern for them. It may well be that all three churches owed their origin to his labors. At any rate, that he was accepted as a spiritual leader in all three seems clear. He obviously felt a personal responsibility for all three groups of believers. His unstinting intercessory labors for all of them provide precious evidence of the true shepherd heart of this man of prayer.

Epaphras stands before us as a challenging example of the ministry of intercession. May the Lord raise up many who follow in his train! Someone has pointed out that he has never seen a church dedicated to "St. Epaphras." Is not that a sad commentary upon the truth that too few Christians have adequately realized the tremendous importance of the ministry of intercession and consequently have failed to appreciate and follow his example? "Epaphras grasped, what many of us are slow to realize, that the tactics of the Christian battle are born of the strategy of prayer."[15]

If the churches in these days are to be victorious, they must find their power on their knees. In a vision a certain man of prayer saw an army coming from a great center of light, bringing light with it wherever it moved. It was arrayed against dense darkness, but as it advanced, the darkness gave way before it. Insignificant in size compared with the force against which it turned, the army conquered wherever it moved. "Invincible" seemed written all over this little host. As the enraptured man looked again, he saw that the army was *advancing on its knees.*

Notes

[1] The word "also" in the KJV lacks adequate textual support and is better omitted.

[2] William Hendriksen, *Exposition of Colossians and Philemon,* New Testament Commentary (Grand Rapids: Baker, 1964), p. 191.

[3] Ralph P. Martin, *Colossians: The Church's Lord and the Christian's Liberty* (Grand Rapids: Zondervan, 1972), p. 144.

[4] John Eadie, *A Commentary on the Greek Text of the Epistle of Paul to the Colossians* (Edinburgh: T & T Clark, 1884), p. 287.

[5] W. H. Griffith Thomas, *Christ Pre-Eminent, Studies in the Epistle to the Colossians* (Chicago: Moody Press, 1923), p. 118.

[6] Thomas, p. 191.

[7] Alexander Maclaren, "The Epistles of St. Paul to the Colossians and Philemon," in *An Exposition of the Bible* (Hartford, Conn.: The S. S. Scranton Co., 1903), 6:286.

[8] Ibid., p. 287.

[9] J. B. Lightfoot, *Saint Paul's Epistles to the Colossians and to Philemon* (1879; reprint ed., London: Macmillan and Co., 1900), p. 238.

[10] Hendriksen, p. 191.

[11] H.C.G. Moule, *The Epistles of Paul the Apostle to the Colossians and to Philemon,* The Cambridge Bible for Schools and Colleges (1893; reprint ed., Cambridge: University Press, 1932), p. 141.

[12] The reading "zeal" in the KJV follows an inferior variant reading.

[13] Martin, p. 145.

[14] E. F. Scott, *The Epistles of Paul to the Colossians, to Philemon, and to the Ephesians,* The Moffatt New Testament Commentary (London: Hodder and Stoughton, 1936), p. 90.

[15] Harrington C. Lee, *St. Paul's Friends* (London: Religious Tract Society, 1918), p. 157.

VIII

The Divine Astonishment

And the Lord saw it, and it displeased him that there was no judgment. And he saw that there was no man, and wondered that there was no intercessor. (Isa. 59:15-16)

Man's failure to avail himself of God's gracious provision to have a share in both the restraint of wickedness and the promotion of righteousness through the ministry of intercession is a definite cause for divine astonishment. That assertion must strike every reader of these words from the pen of Isaiah.

The transgressions of Israel, which had raised a barrier between God and His people, were appalling to contemplate. The nation had become corrupt and openly wicked. Righteousness was in recession and evil was triumphant. And this perversity characteristically found expression in the corruption of human relationships. Justice was being suppressed and perverted, dishonesty prevailed, and bloodshed abounded (vv. 3-7). Yea, the situation had become so desperate that the prophet lamented that "he that departeth from evil maketh himself a prey" (v. 15). This tragic breakdown in social justice was the inevitable consequence of Israel's departure from the living God and violation of its covenant duties.

The perilous moral conditions in Israel lamented by the prophets find striking parallels in many areas of our world today. We too must take warning and realize that persistence in our own evil ways as a nation must bring upon us the same unsparing judgment that befell Israel.

As we are thus led to pause and apply to ourselves the prophet's tragic picture of Israel, our eyes are suddenly drawn above the sordid scene. The prophet shifts his gaze from a wicked world to God above. Above the deplorable human scene, Isaiah sees the inescapable presence of a holy God. His contemplation of God inevitably leads to a declaration of the reaction of Jehovah to the scene: "And the Lord saw it, and it displeased him that there was no judgment. And he saw that there was no man, and wondered that there was no intercessor" (vv. 15-16).

I. *The Occasion for the Divine Astonishment*

The stated occasion for the divine astonishment lay not in the deplorable wickedness of the nation but rather in the fact that such wickedness had not aroused any human intercessor. As we look at the prophet's arresting words, we notice that they form two sentences with two members each. Each statement contains an assertion of God's realization followed by an indication of the divine reaction.

1. *Realization*. "And the Lord saw it." The prophet reminds us that God was not unmindful of the wickedness of the nation. The assertion that Jehovah saw the nation's wickedness embodies a fundamental Biblical truth. We have not an absentee God who has set this world upon its course and then has withdrawn in careless indifference, unmindful of what is going on. The wicked may say in his heart, "God hath forgotten: he hideth his face; he will never see it" (Ps. 10:11), but the fact remains that "the Lord *saw* it."

This is a vital truth that needs to be burned afresh into the conscience of a careless and irreverent generation. Woe to that nation which loses the restraining impact of the consciousness that God is cognizant of all aspects of human life and so boldly plunges into manifold evil. But the omniscient and omnipresent God does see and take notice of the evil as well as the good that men do here on earth. "The eyes of the Lord are in every place, beholding the evil and the good" (Prov. 15:3).

2. *Reaction*. "And it displeased him that there was no judgment." God not only took notice of the evil in Israel, but He also reacted to it. The God revealed in the Bible is not like the gods of the Epicureans, "sitting apart, careless of mankind." He is not

an impassive God, untouched by the feelings of our infirmities. He is a God who reacts to moral conditions, feeling pleasure in goodness and truth and displeasure in the prevalence of injustice and oppression. The sins and iniquities of men grieve and distress His pure heart. He has "no pleasure in the death of the wicked" (Ezek. 33:11), but He does have "pleasure in the prosperity of his servant" (Ps. 35:27).

The moral scene which Jehovah observed was "evil in his eyes" (Young translation),[1] hence stirring His feeling of displeasure. The evil was that there was "no judgment," or "no justice." Let it never be forgotten that injustice in human relations always stirs the Lord's antagonism. God's demand for social justice is in accord with His nature: "the Lord our God will have no part in unrighteousness, or partiality, or the taking of a bribe" (II Chron. 19:7 NASB).

3. *Observation.* "And he saw that there was no man." This assertion connects this second statement closely with the preceding. But now God's attention centers on the human failure to arise in opposition to the evil situation. "What was wanting was not merely a qualified man, but any man whatever, to maintain the cause of Israel and Jehovah."[2] God looked for a champion to arise who would resist the unrighteousness and defend the oppressed. He looked for such a man, but He found none. The prophet Ezekiel recorded a similar situation: "I sought for a man among them, that should make up the hedge, and stand in the gap before me for the land, that I should not destroy it: but I found none" (22:30).

4. *Reaction.* This human failure evoked a strong reaction in the heart of God: "And [He] wondered that there was no intercessor." In view of the desperate need for a man who would stand to champion the cause of truth and justice, God is made to wonder that no one can be found. He wondered that there should be no one like Abraham who interceded before God in behalf of wicked Sodom before divine judgment fell upon it (Gen. 18:22-33).

It is generally agreed that the word "wondered" is too mild to express the force of the original. Delitzsch renders it "and he was astonished,"[3] Alexander uses "he stood aghast,"[4] and Orelli translates it "he was shocked."[5] To be sure, the prophet employs terms of human emotion to describe the divine reaction, but he does so in order that we may better understand the astonishing nature of His reaction. Only in such terms can the prophet adequately picture the divine reaction to the lack of an intercessor in view of the need for such a man. But the expression implies more than mere astonishment; it conveys His active displeasure at the situation.

The term rendered "intercessor" denotes one who intervenes, one who steps in between God and the sinning people to plead on their behalf. It is implied that the evil situation produced an imminent danger which was unavoidable unless someone actively stepped in to avert it.

With reference to how many places and causes in God's kingdom must it not be said with truth and aptness that there is "no intercessor"? It is the burden of this stark reality that the Spirit of God is seeking to impress upon our hearts through this striking revelation by the prophet Isaiah. God is looking for a man who will actively take the place of an intercessor for His cause, and He is amazed that none can be found.

II. *The Reasons for the Divine Astonishment*

Following his picture of the divine astonishment, Isaiah records that as a consequence of His failure to find an intercessor, God prepared to render judgment. Since He found no man to cooperate with Him in praying for the salvation of Israel, He acted directly to vindicate His cause. It is thus clear that God seeks to work through sanctified human agents to accomplish His purpose. It is ever the desire of God to have His saints join Him in the execution of the redemptive program. The repeated failure to enter effectively into this ministry of intercession in furthering the work of the Lord must certainly be a matter of astonishment to God. But we rejoice in the realization that in our Lord Jesus Christ we have the perfect answer to the divine search for a faithful intercessor.

But God still yearns to draw His people into this ministry of intercession and still reacts in astonishment when they fail to avail themselves of the glorious privilege of working with Him through prayer. Why should this common failure evoke God's astonishment? Let us remind ourselves of several reasons.

1. *Scriptural teaching.* Must not God wonder that there are so few intercessors in view of the unequivocal teaching of the Scriptures about intercessory prayer? The Scriptures unmistakably declare and forcefully illustrate the truth that "the effectual fervent prayer of a righteous man availeth much" (James 5:16).

The experiences of Old Testament saints such as Abraham, Moses, Elijah, and Daniel confirm it.

The teaching of Jesus likewise asserts the power and importance of intercession. He thought of prayer as a potent means for the furtherance of the kingdom of God and commanded His disciples to engage in it. Before He sent out the Twelve, as well as the seventy, He commanded them, "Pray ye therefore the Lord of the harvest, that he will send forth labourers into his harvest" (Matt. 9:38; cf. Luke 10:2). In the Upper Room Discourse Jesus affirmed the mighty power of intercessory prayer when He said to His disciples, "He that believeth on me, the works that I do shall he do also; and greater works than these shall he do; because I go unto my Father. And whatsoever ye shall ask in my name, that will I do" (John 14:12-13). These greater works are thus seen to be works accomplished through the power of intercessory prayer.

The example and teaching of the Apostle Paul constitute a ringing challenge to engage in this ministry. His epistles reveal the reality of his own prayer life. He prayed for the churches and called upon them to pray for him and the work of the gospel (Rom. 15:30-32; Eph. 6:18-19; Phil. 1:9-11; Col. 2:1, 4:2-4). He challenged the church to a life of intercession "for all men" (I Tim. 2:1). To him prayer was the connection with the power of God, and he sought to lead others to avail themselves of this power.

Surely no one can read the Scriptures and fail to see the teaching that the ministry of intercession offers a potent means of Christian service in which every believer may engage. Can we who profess to believe and accept the Scriptures as our authority in matters of faith and practice fail to engage in this ministry without bringing upon ourselves the guilt of disobedience to known truth?

2. *Christ's example.* Must not God wonder that there are so few intercessors in view of the fact that our Lord Himself engaged in this ministry while here on earth and is even now continuing it in the presence of the Father (Rom 8:34; Heb. 7:25)? Not only did He teach His disciples to pray the prayer of intercession, but He Himself prayed for others. He said to Peter, "I have prayed for thee, that thy faith fail not" (Luke 22:32). When He was being nailed to the cross He prayed, "Father, forgive them; for they know not what they do" (Luke 23:34). The matchless prayer

recorded in John 17, offered by Jesus in the hearing of His disciples on the night before His crucifixion, provides a beautiful illustration of the ministry of Jesus now "at the right hand of God . . . for us" (Rom. 8:34). Can we who profess to accept Him as Saviour as well as our perfect example (I Pet. 2:21), see Him ever engaged in this ministry of intercession, and ourselves remain indifferent to its practice? Can we escape the conclusion that our failure here must be a cause for divine astonishment?

3. *Great results.* Must not God wonder that there are so few intercessors in view of the fact that His mightiest works are manifested only in the pathway of unselfish and persevering intercession? A study of the great spiritual movements in church history reveals that behind every such movement of revival stood an individual intercessor or a small band of faithful intercessors. The phenomenal missionary labors of David Brainerd among the American Indians in the eighteenth century find their explanation in the agonizing intercessory labors in which he engaged. Prayer was the secret of the revival powers manifested under the ministry of Charles G. Finney–his own prayers and those of others, as, for example, "Father" Nash and Abel Clary. The revival fires that fell in Ireland in 1859 came in answer to the united prayers of a small group of young men upon whom the burden of prayer had been laid. The widespread blessings that flowed from the Fulton Street Prayer Meeting in New York are well known. The mighty revivals that swept around the world under the ministry of R. A. Torrey were undergirded by an intensified wave of intercessory prayer.

The revival in Wales in 1904 and 1905 that swept uncounted multitudes into the kingdom of God was preceded by five years of intense intercessory prayers on the part of a Welsh evangelist named Seth Joshua. Finally the soul travail ceased and calm expectation followed. Then the fire fell and God raised up a young coal miner of the land, Evan Roberts, to become the human leader of the revival.

The revival among the Telugus at Lone Star Mission forms one of the miracles of modern missionary history. The work of the mission was at the point of failure. For years the work had been so unfruitful that the mission board in America had decided to close the station. For the missionary couple on the station the outlook was dark; the only remaining help was in God.

One morning before daybreak the missionary and his wife, Dr. and Mrs. Jowett, with two native servants ascended the hill above Ongole to ask God to save Lone Star Mission and the lost souls of India. They wrestled with God on behalf of a heathen world, like Elijah on Carmel. They prayed in faith, assured that God would answer.

At last the day dawned and the gray streaks were crossing the eastern sky. Just as the sun arose above the horizon, Dr. Jowett arose and seemed to see a great light. Turning his tear-stained face toward the heavens, he declared that he saw the cactus field below transformed into a church and mission buildings. His faith grasped and gripped the great fact. He claimed the promise and challenged God to answer a prayer which was entirely for His own glory and the salvation of men.

The money came almost immediately and clearly from the hand of God. The needed worker came in the person of John Clough, a man of God's choice. Out of his divinely guided work in connection with famine relief, a mighty revival followed. At Ongole, 2,222 were baptized in one day, and 8,000 in six weeks. On that cactus field developed one of the most extensive Christian communities in any field of modern missions.

Surely God has abundantly shown that when men will engage in unselfish, persevering intercession, mighty manifestations of divine power will be given. In view of this fact, must not God wonder that there are so few intercessors among His people today?

4. *World need.* Must not God wonder that there are so few intercessors in view of the insistent call for the exercise of this potent ministry arising from the needs of a world steeped in sin? From every side reports crash in on us of heart-rending tragedy and fearful need. The sensitive soul is almost overwhelmed with the awful realization of unfathomable human need the world over. We can readily join in the poignant words of E. P. Alldredge when he exclaims:

World need! World need! World need!
How we feel, dear God, the full urge of it,
And the swing and the swirl and the surge of it,
    The distress of it,
    The dire press of it;
And the pall and the thrall and the call
That comes now from the great and the small.

World need! World need! World need!
How we feel, dear God, the dread chill of it,
And the dearth and the death and the debt of it;
 The vast sweep of it,
 The great deep of it;
And the wear and the tear and the care
That breaks now the sad hearts everywhere!

The temptation is ever to allow ourselves to become hardened to these pressing needs and to go on our own self-centered way without being moved to intercessory prayer for needy ones all around us. The Holy Spirit is seeking to make the desperate world conditions an insistent call on our hearts for prayer. Prayer is the primary need. In the efforts of the churches today to respond to these vast needs, the most urgent need is not money, important as it is. Nor is it the need for better plans and organizations, important as these are. Nor yet is the primary need the demand for more workers, paramount as that may seem. Behind all of these needs, and others, is the basic need for more Spirit-empowered intercessors. If this need were adequately met, all these other needs would soon be supplied.

The needs of a world lost in sin caused God in love to give His only begotten Son to redeem mankind. Can we who have experienced God's redeeming love in our own lives continue to be indifferent to the Spirit's call for intercessory prayer on behalf of a dying world? If we fail to answer that call, will we be surprised if God expresses His amazement?

5. *Personal failure.* Must not God wonder that there are so few intercessors in view of the fact that so many of us know that we could and should be intercessors, and yet are not? To be sure there are believers who have not yet been brought to a realization of this mighty ministry of intercession. They need to be led into a definite understanding of the limitless possibilities of the life of intercession. But many others of us have been led to see the truth about this ministry, have acknowledged the need for it, have seen the greatness of its scope and power, and yet we have failed adequately to engage in it. We cannot plead the excuse of ignorance.

We must humbly bow in contrition and acknowledge our guilt. We have failed! We hear the divine lament concerning the lack of an intercessor and within the recesses of our own consciousness there arises a figure which condemns us with the words, "Thou art the man!" As we bow before the Lord, let us penitently seek His forgiveness and earnestly beseech Him to fill our hearts with a great yearning and a resolute determination to enter more fully into this mighty ministry of working by prayer. Let us pray with the poet:

Make me an Intercessor,
One who can really pray,
One of "the Lord's remembrancers"
By night as well as day.

Make me an Intercessor
Through whom the Spirit can plead
For sin and sorrow on every side.
For men in darkness and need.

Make me an Intercessor,
In spirit-touch with Thee,
And given the heavenly vision,
Pray through to victory.

Make me an Intercessor;
O teach me how to prevail,
To stand my ground and still pray on,
Though powers of hell assail.

Make me an Intercessor,
Sharing Thy death and life;
In prayer be claiming for others
The vict'ry in the strife.

Make me an Intercessor,
And willing for deeper death;
Yes, emptied, broken, and then made anew,
And filled with living breath.

Make me an Intercessor,
Hidden–unknown–set apart,
Thought little of by those around,
But satisfying Thy heart.

Notes

[1]Robert Young, *The Holy Bible Consisting of the Old and New Covenants Translated According to the Letter and Idioms of the Original Languages* (London: Pickering & Inglis, n.d.).

[2]Joseph Addison Alexander, *Commentary on the Prophecies of Isaiah* (1875; reprint ed., Grand Rapids: Zondervan, 1953), 2:370.

[3]Franz Delitzsch, *Biblical Commentary on the Prophecies of Isaiah,* trans. James Martin (Reprint ed., Grand Rapids: Eerdmans, 1949), 2:403.

[4]Alexander, 2:370.

[5]G. Von Orelli, *The Prophecies of Isaiah,* trans. J. S. Banks (Edinburgh: T & T Clark, 1895), p. 317.

IX

Wanted–A Man!

And I sought for a man among them, that should make up the hedge, and stand in the gap before me for the land, that I should not destroy it: but I found none. Therefore have I poured out mine indignation upon them. (Ezek. 22:30-31)

The urgent need is for a man who will stand in the gap between a sinful world and the impending judgment of God. God desires to avoid exercising a just and deserved punishment upon an apostate nation; yet He finds Himself ''helpless'' without such a man. That is the solemn assertion in the words of this text, spoken by God Himself through the mouth of His prophet Ezekiel.

It is as though the eternal God Himself has hung out His sign in the window of heaven: *Wanted–A Man*. But the startling fact is that after He has left the sign there for a considerable time, He has to lament that there have been no applicants for the job. And since He has found no one to fill the needed position, God announces that He can no longer withhold judgment.

Israel had fallen into a state of national apostasy; conditions were shocking indeed. Sin and corruption were rampant on every hand, threatening inevitable doom. The need of the hour was for a man who could avert the impending catastrophe.

Conditions in our world today are likewise grim and appalling. Surely in this day God is still looking for a man. Had we but the spiritual vision of the prophet, we too might behold in heaven's window God's sign: *Wanted–A Man*.

I. *The Divine Search* (v. 30a)

The declarative statement "And I sought for a man among them" (v. 30) are the words of God Himself. It is not a man looking for God, but rather God looking for a man. God is searching for the man necessary to meet the crucial situation of the hour. The key to the world's need is a real man, and the ultimate answer to that need will be found when God Himself acts in bringing the man Jesus Christ back to this world.

The fundamental fact of human history is that God is looking for a man rather than man looking for God. Some theologians—motivated by an optimistic, un-Scriptural view of human nature—have endeavored to interpret human history as the record of man's progressive discovery of God. They have painted a rosy picture of man's gradual rise to higher and higher levels of intellectual, social, and moral achievements until, at last, in some distant future, man will eventually come into a full realization of his inherent dignity as a son of God. It is a beautiful and alluring picture. There is only one thing wrong with this scene–*it is not true.*

Sinful man is not looking for God; rather, he is trying hard to get away from God. That has been true ever since man fell into sin and thereby became estranged from God. When Adam and Eve sinned in the Garden of Eden, we would have expected them to have cried out, "Oh, God, where are You? We have sinned! We have sinned!" But nothing of the kind happened. As fallen creatures they did not seek God, but rather they sought to hide from God when He came to them.

The history of mankind is not a gradual ascent to God but instead a winding path that leads deeper into the gloom of death and despair. As a sinful creature, man naturally seeks to hide from a holy God. In describing sinful man's history, Paul records that men "did not like to retain God in their knowledge" (Rom. 1:28). Rejecting the revelation of God that they did have, men corrupted their knowledge of Him and went further and further away from God.

Near the turn of the nineteenth century, F. W. Farrar wrote a popular book entitled *Seekers After God.* A certain western bookseller had a number of requests for the volume but had no copies available. He sent a telegram to the dealers in New York requesting them to ship him a number of the books. After a while a telegram came back which read, "NO SEEKERS AFTER GOD IN NEW YORK. TRY PHILADELPHIA."

Whenever an individual seeks God, it is because God first began the search. It was the shepherd who sought the lost sheep, not the lost sheep the shepherd. A lost sheep cannot find its way back to the fold; it must be found by the shepherd. "The Son of man is come to seek and to save that which was lost" (Luke 19:10). The sinful human must first be drawn by God before he can come to God. Jesus said, "No man can come to me, except the Father which hath sent me draw him" (John 6:44).

But in the passage before us God is not looking for a sinner, but for a saint. God here is looking for the man whom He can use to carry out His saving purpose for the nation of Israel. He is looking for the saint who will voluntarily surrender himself to the call of God's service.

II. *The Divine Purpose* (v. 30b)

God clearly states His purpose in searching for a man: "I sought for a man among them, that should make up the hedge, and stand in the gap before me for the land" (v. 30). God sees an urgent need, and He is looking for the man whom He can use to fill that need. This need is indicated under two figures of speech, yet the need for a man is the same in both.

1. *To "make up the hedge."* God had graciously placed a hedge, or wall, around His people for their protection. Satan complained before God that He had placed a protective hedge around Job so that he could not be touched (Job 1:10). But the prevailing corruption of the nation was breaking down the hedge which Jehovah had placed around His people and had created a serious breach, just as sin always tears down the protective wall around a people or a nation. To allow the breach in God's hedge around Israel to remain unclosed was to invite the destruction of the nation. Through that breach catastrophe was about to strike in devastating judgment. God was looking for a man who would be able to close the breach by leading the people to repent and turn from their evil ways.

Serious breaches have likewise been made in the moral and spiritual defenses of our own nation. As we behold the tide of crime and lawlessness in our land we wonder how long judgment can be averted. In Chapter 35 of his massive and masterful work *The Decline and Fall of the Roman Empire* (1787), Edward Gibbon concluded that the primary causes of the downfall of the once mighty Roman Empire were not *external* but *internal*. After sketching the breakdown of social order in the empire, the increasingly oppressive Roman system of taxation, the spendthrift practices of both government and private citizen, Gibbon wrote, "If all the barbarian conquerors had been annihilated in the same hour, their total destruction would not have restored the empire of the West." As we read Gibbon's assessment in the light of prevailing conditions in our own land, we are compelled in all seriousness to ask ourselves, Will history repeat itself? Where are the men who will act to close up the breaches before well-deserved judgment falls?

2. *To "stand in the gap before me for the land."* Here the figure is altered somewhat. There is the continued recognition of the dangerous breach which needs to be closed, but now the emphasis is upon the man needed to fill that gap. Evil is pouring into the nation through the gap, and a man willing and able to intervene must fill it to arrest the flood of sin and corruption. The people of God must forsake the sins which are causing the gap and return to the divine laws and godly practices which they have forsaken.

The filling of the gap is essentially a spiritual task. It will not be closed merely by appropriate legislation, good and desirable as that may be. Nor will it be closed by the inauguration of new schemes and programs which leave untouched the underlying problem of human sinfulness. Since it is, in reality, a matter of sin arrogantly flaunting its triumph in the face of a holy God, God looked for a man "who could stand before me in the breach to defend the land from ruin" (NEB). The solution to the situation does not lie simply on the human level. The task of standing in the gap to arrest the onrushing evil is essentially a matter of prayer and intercession. Keil believes that in this passage "the intercession of Abraham for Sodom (Gen. xviii. 13 sqq.) was floating before the mind of Ezekiel."[1] He holds that the primary significance of this call for one "to stand in the gap" is not a call for the man's personal interposition against the evils but rather a call to "avert the judgment of destruction by his intercession."[2] Fausset remarks that the expression is the "image for interceding between the people and God (Genesis 20:7; Exodus 32:11; Numbers 16:48)."[3] Moses thus stood in the gap when he made intercession for Israel to turn away the wrath of God (Ps. 106:23). Through intercession God begins to work and the tide of evil is stayed. But thus to stand in the gap is difficult work and requires a soul having the courage that comes through being yielded and devoted to God.

Charles G. Finney was conducting a revival in a certain town. During those meetings a young woman came from a neighboring town and begged him to come and hold meetings in her community, her voice choked with deep emotion as she made her request. But because of the heavy demands on him, Finney told her that he did not see how he could go. Aroused by the earnestness of the young woman, Finney made inquiry about the community from which she came and found that it was a veritable spiritual wilderness, cursed by a preacher who had turned to infidelity.

When the young woman came again the next Sunday with her request and appeared so much affected that she could hardly converse, Finney promised to go. The next Sunday afternoon when he arrived at the home of the young woman, he heard her praying in the room above. Following the evening service, he spent the night in her home and during most of that night he heard her weeping and interceding in her room.

The next morning she pled with Finney to come back. He came again, and at the next meeting a revival broke out, and nearly all the principal inhabitants of the place were saved. The result was that the moral atmosphere of the community was transformed. Behind that revival was a young woman who had deliberately placed herself in the gap before God until it was closed.

III. *The Divine Intention* (v. 30c)

God explicitly declares His gracious intention in thus looking for a man to stand in the gap before Him on behalf of the land. It was "that I should not destroy it" (v. 30). The stated intention reveals the compassionate heart of God; He desired to show mercy to sinning Israel if possible. Through the gap in the protective wall, the good was running out and massive evils were flooding in, plunging the nation into darkness and corruption. Unless the gap was soon closed God must break in with judgment. The clouds of judgment were heavy over Israel, but God would rather bless than blight. He was loath to rush through the breach with destruction. He yearned to find someone who would stand in the gap so that judgment might be averted.

God was looking for a man who would cooperate with Him in His saving purpose. "Through the plan of prayer," Billheimer observes, "God actually is inviting redeemed man into FULL partnership with Him, not in *making* the divine decisions, but in *implementing* those decisions in the affairs of humankind."[4]

Through intercessory prayer God is giving His saints the glorious opportunity of working with Him in the defeat of evil and the triumph of righteousness.

The tragic conditions in Israel, vividly portrayed by Ezekiel in the preceding verses (22:24-29), demanded swift judgment from above. The sins of the nation demanded sweeping judgment, but the heart of God yearned for a man who loved God and who would through prevailing prayer throw himself unreservedly into the breach to turn the tide and stem the flood of iniquity.

IV. *The Divine Lament* (v. 30d)

In view of God's gracious intention to spare the land if He could find the needed man, how heart-rending His lament, "but I found none." This solemn assertion does not strictly mean that there was not a single righteous man left in Jerusalem, for Jeremiah, Baruch, and some others were there. But the Lord's statement "I sought for a man *among them*" has specific reference to the different classes enumerated in verses 25-29 above. Among the conspiring prophets, the compromising priests, the profiteering princes, and the oppressing landlords, God found not a single individual who was morally able to exercise the work of an intercessor. Those in positions of leadership and influence in a nation carry a heavy moral responsibility before God.

How important is the man whom God can use! "Had one real man been found to reprove the people, restore religious worship, and plead with God, Israel might have been spared its overthrow."[5] The influence of one man can shape the destiny of a nation. The intercession of Moses for the calf-worshipping Israelites at Mount Sinai saved them from extinction (Exod. 32:7-14). Samuel stood in the gap before God for the people and prevailed in intercession, and the course of the nation was turned Godward (I Sam. 7:3-13). One wonders what might have become of Israel in captivity had there not been a Daniel who took the sins of the nation upon himself and fervently pled with God for the restoration of the nation in accordance with the divine promise (Dan. 9:2-23). The presence of Paul on a doomed ship resulted in the deliverance of the whole crew from death (Acts 27:22-25). Luther's firm faith brought deliverance, both spiritual and temporal, to Europe and changed the course of history. God found His man in the person of John Wesley, and England was spared the horrors of the French Revolution.

Who can calculate the irreparable losses that have resulted from the lack of the needed man in the critical hours of history? How shall we measure the losses suffered by the Church because it did not call out intercessors to cry unceasingly to God for their friends, community, nation, and, above all, a lost world? How God must grieve over a lukewarm Church which is so indifferent to this urgent need for unceasing intercession! God is looking for a man big enough and strong enough to hold up this sinful world in prayer and bind it to His throne by golden chains of unceasing intercession.

Such prevailing intercessors are hard to find, as they were in the days of ancient Israel. Indeed, they have always been hard to find. Christians readily acknowledge the importance of prayer, but, sadly, few are willing to pay the price of unremitting intercession.

If *you* knew that a pagan man
   Was lying at death's door,
Would *you* not drop your work awhile
   And for his soul implore?

If *you* your missionary friend
   Could see all impotent and ill,
Would *you* grudge him an hour of prayer
   So he his place could fill?

"No, no! A thousand 'nos'," you say.
   Yet each day that goes by
These things prevail in heathen lands–
   One hundred thousand die!

But days slip by and weeks and months,
   You've had no time to pray;
So missionaries must come home:
   The Enemy holds sway.

Ah, cowards we–we will not go
   Nor labor on in prayer,
Nor give as He has prospered us;
   I ask you, Is that fair?

What if the order were reversed,
   And no one cared for you,
While lost in heathen night you cried,
   "Oh, come and tell us, too!"

                   –Betty Honeywell

V. *The Divine Retribution* (v. 31a)

"Therefore have I poured out mine indignation upon them" (v. 31a). Oh, that terrible "therefore." How it should grip our souls and spur us to action! Because God could find no man to stand in the gap, He poured out His wrath upon a sinful land. The judgment fell by moral necessity. For long God had withheld His judgment, but at last the destruction came. Sin persisted in brings inescapable doom.

The storms of divine judgment are hovering on the world's horizon. Whether the hour of judgment will be restrained yet longer depends on whether God can find His man to stand in the gap. May God arouse us to a realization of the seriousness of our times. The hour is desperate–can we continue to behold the seriousness of the world scene and sit prayerlessly by?

> The world looks out of weary eyes,
>   The burdens crush, the cares perplex;
> The sun shines out of somber skies,
>   The hopes of many lie in wrecks.
> How can we help the world today?
> Take time to pray. Take time to pray.
>
> Look o'er the world and see the need.
>   Look out on suff'ring everywhere.
> God waits for saints to intercede;
>   God's work awaits our earnest prayer.
> And shall we fail our God today?
> Take time to pray. Take time to pray.
>
> When stoutest hearts are filled with dread,
>   When want and suff'ring are so great,
> When children die for lack of bread,
>   When all the world seems full of hate–
> God help us! Can we turn away?
> Take time to pray! Take time to pray!
>
> –Jennie E. Shephardson

Notes

[1]Carl Friedrich Keil, *Biblical Commentary on the Prophecies of Ezekiel,* trans. James Martin (Grand Rapids: Eerdmans, 1950), 1:320.

[2]Ibid., p. 319.

[3]Robert Jamieson and A. R. Fausset, *A Commentary, Critical and Explanatory, on the Old Testament,* vol. 1, *Old Testament* (Hartford, Conn.: The S. S. Scranton Co., n.d.), p. 595.

[4]Paul E. Billheimer, *Destined for the Throne* (Fort Washington, Pa.: Christian Literature Crusade, 1975), p. 46. Italics by Billheimer.

[5]E. H. Plumptre, ''The Book of the Prophet Ezekiel,'' in *The Pulpit Commentary* (Reprint ed., Chicago: Wilcox and Follet Co., n.d.), 2:12.

X

Learning to Pray from Daniel

*And I set my face unto the Lord God, to seek by prayer and
supplications, with fasting, and sackcloth, and ashes: And I
prayed unto the Lord my God, and made my confession.*
(Dan. 9:3-4)

The book of Daniel presents an amazing demonstration of the
reality of working by prayer. The experiences of Daniel the
prophet offer startling proof of the far-reaching consequences of
a vital ministry of intercession. His experiences provide indubi-
table evidence of the strategic importance of prayer as a means
of promoting the cause of righteousness in the raging conflict
with the forces of spiritual iniquity. The prayer ministry of Daniel
is a challenging example for believers today.

Daniel was one of the truly great men of the Old Testament.
He was a man who consistently rose above the sordidness of his
environment. His life was marked by a spirit of personal humility,
vigorous faith in God, scrupulous faithfulness in the fulfillment
of executive duties, and profound insight and spiritual understanding. The very loftiness of his character lifted him above the level
of his contemporaries. Of all men appearing in the Old Testament,
Daniel appears as one of the most blameless and pure.

The secret of Daniel's personal excellence and his high at-
tainments, as well as the abiding spiritual impact of his life, must
be found in his life of prayer and unswerving devotion to God.
He had mastered the secret of working with God by prayer. The

book of Daniel refers to his praying in connection with no fewer than four of the momentous events in his life (chaps. 2, 6, 9, 10). His prayer of confession and intercession recorded in the ninth chapter is one of the truly great prayers of the Bible.

I. *The Character of His Praying*

The references to the praying of Daniel furnish instructive lessons concerning the characteristics of effective praying.

1. *Prayer practices.* The record makes it clear that Daniel had learned the value of a regular *time* and *place* for prayer. He was systematic and methodical in his prayer life.

Daniel observed regular prayer periods. From 6:10 we learn that it was his practice to pray three times a day. This was his established practice–"as he did aforetime." Daniel had put into practice the resolve of King David, "Evening, and morning, and at noon, will I pray, and cry aloud" (Ps. 55:17). Daniel had deliberately arranged to give prayer a definite and systematic place in his strenuous life, and he carefully adhered to these three daily prayer periods. He must have faced the temptation to allow the duties of his active life as a government official to interfere with his prayer times; yet he resolutely resisted the tantalizing temptations to let other duties rob him of his time with God.

Daniel had learned to appreciate and to utilize the value of regularity in prayer. He had cultivated the habit of turning to God at regular periods. It is a common observation that those who have no regular habits of prayer very seldom do much praying. It is well for God's people purposefully and deliberately to set aside and faithfully adhere to a definite prayer schedule. Believers thus recognize prayer as an important part of the Christian life and give it the place which it deserves. It was this practice that made Daniel a "man of his times" in the truest sense.

Daniel's prayer habit stood him in good stead in the hour of crisis. Prayer for him was not just an emergency measure to be resorted to in time of need. His prayer habits enabled him to "find grace to help in time of need" (Heb. 4:16). Those who do not cultivate the practice of regular prayer may find that their praying does not sustain them in the hour of crisis.

Daniel's prayer habits naturally led him to establish a regular place for prayer. The believer's communion with God is not restricted to any specific time or place; yet a regular place for prayer is helpful and highly desirable. Jesus assumed the possession of

such a place when He instructed His disciples: "When thou pray-
est, enter into *thy* closet, and when thou hast shut *thy* door, pray
to thy Father" (Matt. 6:6).

Daniel found such a place for prayer in his own residence.
During the early years of his life in Babylon, Daniel's "house"
(2:17) apparently was an official residence for the king's servants;
the context indicates that Daniel shared his quarters with his three
Hebrew companions. It was there that they united in praying that
God would make known to them Nebuchadnezzar's forgotten
dream. Their conviction that they could gain an audience with
"the God of heaven" (2:18) in the privacy of their residence was
gloriously confirmed.

In later life, as an important government official, Daniel had
his place of prayer in his house where "in his roof chamber he
had windows open toward Jerusalem" (6:10 NASB). He had
chosen an apartment raised above the flat roof of his home as the
place for his fellowship with God, a place more removed and less
liable to disturbance than his usual living quarters. Its open windows, not covered with lattice-work, enabled him in his prayers
to look toward Jerusalem as the place where God had placed His
Name. His place of prayer clearly was a sacred place for Daniel.

Daniel's prayer life was an open acknowledgment of his dependence upon God. He knew the value of united prayer as well
as individual prayer. When the rash edict of a furious Nebuchadnezzar that all the wise men of Babylon should be executed (2:12)
placed the life of Daniel and his three companions in great danger
(2:13), Daniel united his friends in prayer to God to reveal to
them the king's dream so that they should not be destroyed with
the rest of the wise men of Babylon (2:17-18). Dennett asserts,
"It is the first instance of united prayer recorded in Scripture;
and the fact that these children of the captivity resorted to it,
discovers to us the secret of their holy and separate walk."[1] The
story in chapter 6 demonstrates that Daniel also resorted to prayer
when his individual life was at stake.

2. *Prayer elements.* The example of Daniel as a man of prayer
makes clear a number of the elements of effective prayer.

In his praying Daniel manifested a becoming attitude of *reverence* and humility. Upon entering his prayer chamber, Daniel
"kneeled upon his knees" (6:10), thus assuming "a physical attitude that was a picture of his spiritual attitude when he approached

Almighty God."[2] His posture was indicative of an attitude of humility, reverence, and submission to God. The Scriptures repeatedly mention kneeling as the characteristic posture of the supplicant before God (I Kings 8:54; Ezra 9:5; Luke 22:41; Acts 7:60, 9:40, 21:5; Eph. 3:14).

The Scriptures do not prescribe any definite posture in prayer, however, and varied postures in prayer are mentioned. Beside kneeling, reference is also made to standing (I Kings 8:22; Mark 11:25), bowing down (Ps. 95:6), sitting (II Sam. 7:18), and falling on the face (Num. 16:22; Josh. 5:14; Matt. 26:39). There is thus no hard-and-fast command in Scripture concerning the posture to be taken in prayer. Physical posture does not determine the attitude of the heart, but it may definitely aid it. Of importance is the attitude of reverent dependence upon God.

A spirit of *earnest persistence* characterized the praying of Daniel. In 6:11 it is recorded of Daniel that he continued "praying and making supplication before his God"; in 9:3 he set his face unto the Lord God, seeking an answer "by prayer and supplications, with fasting, and sackcloth, and ashes"; and in 10:2-3 he continued his disciplined quest for three whole weeks until the divine answers arrived. His praying was earnest and persistent, deeply fervent and intense, marked by sacrifice and self-abnegation. Prayer for him was not merely a matter of using the right terms but a vital heart concern.

A little boy, a member of a Sunday school in Jamaica, called upon the missionary and stated that he had lately been very ill and in his sickness had often wished that the missionary had been present to pray for him. "But, Thomas," said the missionary, "I hope you prayed for yourself."

"Oh, yes, sir; I did," was the reply.

"Did you repeat any of the prayers I taught you?"

"No, sir," answered the lad.

"Well, how did you pray then?" asked the missionary.

"Why, sir, I just begged."

Whenever in our praying we become so serious that we are willing to deny ourselves the luxuries–even the ordinary necessities–of life, and in deep travail of soul we persistently plead before God for His answers, we can be sure that He will answer. Our praying is often so ineffectual because it costs us so little.

Even in the hour of crisis, Daniel's praying was marked by *thanksgiving:* "When Daniel knew that the writing was signed, . . . he kneeled upon his knees three times a day, and prayed, and gave thanks before his God, as he did aforetime" (6:10). He did not forget to thank his God for all the past mercies and benefits he had received, even though his dangerous circumstances at the time were very far from causing a feeling of thanksgiving. Daniel also gave fervent thanks for the answers to prayer received. When in answer to prayer the forgotten dream of Nebuchadnezzar was made known to Daniel, his first response was heartfelt thanksgiving to God (2:19-23).

Thanksgiving is a vital element in true prayer. God plainly exhorts His people to unite thanksgiving with their prayers (Phil. 4:6; I Thess. 5:17-18). The practice of thanksgiving is vital for a happy Christian life, for the thankful heart will have no time for murmuring or complaining.

> When thou hast thanked thy God
>   For every blessing sent,
> But little time will then remain
>   For murmur or lament.

It is not enough to feel thankful for blessings received; there must be a definite expression of our thanks to God. "Oh that men would praise the Lord for his goodness, and for his wonderful works to the children of men" (Ps. 107:8). A kind uncle who had just returned from Paris gave his little niece a beautiful French doll. "And did you thank uncle for the beautiful present?" asked the mother. "Yes, Mamma," was the reply, but then honesty caught up with her, and she added, "but I did not tell him so." Is that the way we treat our Lord when we are the recipients of His wonderful gifts?

The praying of Daniel was also characterized by a spirit of *confession.* This is clearly seen in the striking prayer of the prophet recorded in chapter nine. His prayer contains repeated confession of sin, such as "Whiles I was speaking, and praying, and confessing my sin and the sin of my people Israel" (9:20). Notice the order, first his own sin and then that of the people. The Bible nowhere records any sin in the personal life of Daniel; yet in this prayer he confessed his own sin. He had a true knowledge of his own nature. He knew the sinfulness of his own inner being and was not too proud to confess it.

Once when Alexander Whyte was addressing a small audience, he astonished them by saying that he had found out the name of the most sinful man in Edinburgh and had come to tell them. Then, bending forward, he whispered, "His name is Alexander Whyte!" Having looked into his own heart and confessed what he found there, Whyte was able to speak with power. Such a confession is a humiliating experience but necessary for effective prayer and Christian service. It is a paradox of the Christian life that the closer the saint lives to God the more conscious he becomes of his own sinfulness. Those who live most fully in the light of God's holiness are the ones who are the most conscious of their own unworthiness.

Daniel's confession of his own sinfulness effectively enabled him to identify himself with the sinful people for whom he prayed. "It is only as we ourselves are truly humbled before God that we can humble ourselves for His people. Through grace, and the power of the Holy Spirit, we must put ourselves morally into the circumstances of those whose cause we desire to present to God."[3]

Daniel's praying was also marked by an attitude of *expectancy*. He fully believed that God could and did answer the prayers of His people. When the wise men of Babylon failed to make known Nebuchadnezzar's forgotten dream, and the furious king ordered their destruction (2:1-13), Daniel asked the king for time with the assurance that "he would shew the king the interpretation" (2:16). Daniel and his three companions confidently asked God to reveal the king's dream to them, and their expectancy was rewarded (2:18-19). In chapter 10 this attitude of expectancy enabled Daniel to continue praying for three full weeks until the answer came.

This spirit of expectancy is often sadly lacking in our praying. In the beautiful parabolic story "Expectation Corners," the author relates the story of a king who prepared a city for some of his poor subjects. Not far from them were large storehouses. There everything they could need was supplied if they would but send in their requests. There was but one condition—that they should be on the lookout for the answer so that when the king's messengers came with the answers to their petitions, they should always be found waiting and ready to receive them. The story tells of one despairing person who never expected to get what he asked, because he was too unworthy. One day he was taken to the king's storehouse, and there, to his amazement, he saw stacks of packages addressed to him, all undelivered because the messengers had found his door closed; he was not on the lookout for them. Certainly this parable has its counterpart in the lives of many of God's people today. We do not receive the answers to our prayers because we do not expect them.

3. *Prayer basis.* Daniel's practice of praying with his windows opened toward Jerusalem was prompted by his desire to be Biblical. The practice was rooted in the prayer of Solomon at the dedication of the temple, when he prayed that if God's people should be carried away captive because of their sins and there repent and pray toward "the city which thou hast chosen, and the house which I have built for thy name: then hear thou their prayer and their supplication in heaven thy dwelling place, and maintain their cause" (I Kings 8:48-49). Since the Lord had said to Solomon, "I have heard thy prayer and thy supplication, that thou hast made before me" (I Kings 9:3), Daniel was thus assured that his approach to God would be acceptable.

Daniel also grounded his petitions in the Word of God, as clearly seen in 9:1-2 where we learn that Daniel's great prayer in that chapter arose out of his study of Jeremiah's prophecy. From Jeremiah 25:11-12 he learned that God had promised that the Babylonian captivity was to last for seventy years, and he saw that the seventy years of that prophecy had nearly run out. By faith he accepted the revelation given to Jeremiah and, using it as his basis, began to pray accordingly. This prophecy of Jeremiah "so far from leading the watchful servant of God to assume that the event will automatically transpire without prayer to heaven, calls him to the more extraordinary engagement in prayer."[4] Fully aware that Israel had been sent into captivity because of its sins, Daniel realized that penitent supplications would be a necessary spiritual condition for their restoration from exile. (Cf. Jer. 50:4-5; Ezek. 36:37.) Conscious of the impenitence and unbelief of his people in exile, Daniel personally assumed the attitude of penitence and supplication which Jeremiah had indicated as appropriate for the people. Having learned God's will from the Scriptures, Daniel could pray with assurance and power for its accomplishment. Daniel practiced Bible-based praying.

Here is a basic ingredient of effective prayer. In I John 5:14-15 we read, "And this is the confidence that we have in him, that, if we ask any thing according to his will, he heareth us: and if we know that he hear us, whatsoever we ask, we know that we have the petitions that we desired of him.'' Prayer in accordance with the will of God is sure of an answer. Such prayer is the believer's ratification of God's will; it brings him into active cooperation with God in the furthering of God's will.

We must learn to use the Bible as the guide for our praying. Prayer nourished and guided by the Word of God will be effective. George Mueller, a noted man of prayer, used this secret. For some years he had followed the custom of praying first and then reading the Bible, with no special connection between the two. Then he was led to turn the process completely around; after a word of invocation to have the Spirit's teaching, he now spent hours pouring over the Word, filling himself with the living Word of God; after this, in the very mind of Christ which he had thus received, he poured out praise, prayer, and supplication in great fullness and assurance.

All parts of the inspired Word yield valuable lessons for prayer to an open and yielded heart. The diligent, believing student marvels how fully God has revealed His will in His Word. The prayers of the Bible offer a rich course of instruction, with the prayers of the Apostle Paul especially giving invaluable guidance for effective intercession. But all Scripture is priceless in helping the believer discover what the will of God is. Let us read the newspapers to stimulate in us a sense of the need for prayer, but let us read the Bible that we may be directed to pray aright.

II. *The Cost of His Praying*

The book of Daniel clearly reveals the high cost of effective praying. Daniel experienced the cost of victorious praying in three areas of his life.

1. *Personal purity.* The success of Daniel's prayer life was rooted in his resolute determination to maintain his personal purity and his maintenance of rigid self-discipline. At the commencement of his career in Babylon, Daniel, as a devout young Hebrew, resolved not to defile himself by acquiescing to the idolatrous dietary practices of Babylon (1:8), and as an old man he voluntarily practiced rigid self-discipline for three whole weeks in his diet until he received the answer to his prayer (10:1-3).

When as a young man Daniel was taken to Babylon to be trained for service in the king's court, he "purposed in his heart that he would not defile himself with the portion of the king's meat'' (1:8). This initial test was crucial for the devout young Hebrew. As a dietary matter, to us the test may appear to be of little significance, but for Daniel it was ''the crisis in his life, which was safely passed, otherwise we probably would never have heard of him again.''⁵ For Daniel and his associates the test ''arose doubtless from the heathenish custom of consecrating each meal, by offering a portion to the gods.''⁶ As a devout Hebrew, living according to the demands of the Mosaic law, he could not partake of these meals and retain an undefiled conscience. He resolutely determined not to pollute his conscience by compromise in the matter. God graciously opened up a way for Daniel to retain his purity. It has been noted that his ''unflinching decision perfectly blended with refined courtesy in Daniel.''⁷ His gracious yet unwavering resolve to follow the path of separation was the basis for his later greatness.

He who honors the Lord by a conscientious adherence to His Word in what men may lightly call ''inconsequential matters'' or ''minor details'' is thereby laying the groundwork for the day when the Lord will be able to entrust him with great spiritual opportunities and responsibilities. The conscientious believer will refuse to play loose with what some may consider nonessentials in the Scriptures. The only way in which he can advance in the truth of God and grow in personal holiness is to maintain a good conscience in every area of life. To allow one thing in our life which we know to be contrary to God's will to go unjudged is to set our feet in the path of spiritual decline.

From chapter 10 we learn that when he was an old man, Daniel still practiced rigid self-discipline as a means of gaining a prayer victory. For ''three full weeks'' Daniel mourned, refrained from all dainties, and restricted his diet to the simplest food as he persisted in his prayer quest before God, refusing to give up until the answer came (10:1-3). He voluntarily abstained from the enjoyments of life in order to give himself wholly to his spiritual quest. A self-indulgent, pleasure-loving individual cannot be a prevailing prayer warrior.

2. *Official faithfulness.* Success in prayer also enacts a high cost in our relations to others. Daniel's prayer life was consonant with the fact of his unimpeachable integrity and unwavering fidelity in the performance of his official duties (6:4). He refused

to stoop to any unworthy relations with king or state (5:17; 6:22). There was no negligence in the performance of his public duties; neither did he resort to questionable, self-serving practices as a government leader.

The holiness of his life and the unassailable integrity of his official conduct rebuked the corruption of those officials who sought to enrich their own coffers at the expense of the government. Tatford observes, "As much later in the case of our Lord, the very perfection demonstrated only served to increase the hatred of those who were conscious of their own guilt."[8] Their bitter hatred led them to concoct a clever scheme to destroy Daniel. It was his sense of perfect innocence in relation to his scheming colleagues and the deluded king that enabled Daniel to continue fearlessly his prayer practice in the face of impending destruction.

We cannot have unworthy relations or dealings with others, whether Christians or non-Christians, and expect answers to our prayers. Moral integrity in all our dealings with others is a condition for effective praying. "First be reconciled to thy brother, and then come and offer thy gift" (Matt. 5:24).

3. *Godward allegiance.* Daniel's exploits in prayer were grounded in his unwavering loyalty to God. He had given his supreme allegiance to God, and he allowed nothing to turn him from it.

The only charge which the enemies of Daniel could raise against him was his faithfulness to God, misinterpreted as disobedience to the king's command (6:13). By a cunning appeal to the king's vanity, Daniel's enemies had tricked Darius into signing a decree forbidding all prayer for thirty days except to the king alone. The diabolical plot maliciously produced for Daniel a conflict between his loyalty to God and his loyalty to the state. Confronted with this conflict, Daniel deliberately refused to let the king take the place of God in his life. "Now when Daniel knew that the writing was signed, he went into his house; and his windows being open in his chamber toward Jerusalem, he kneeled upon his knees three times a day, and prayed, and gave thanks before his God, as he did aforetime" (6:10). His continuance of his regular prayer practice was not an ostentatious display; as formerly, he simply continued to pray in his prayer chamber on the roof of his own house. Daniel's enemies detected his continued praying at once because they were spying on him. He might have closed his windows to avoid being seen, but that act would have been compromise and cowardice. By his action Daniel clearly revealed where his loyalty lay. He resolved to be true to God at any cost. Calvin observes, "God requires not only faith in the heart and the inward affections, but also the witness and confession of our piety."[9] Daniel doubtless knew that he was being watched, but instead of looking at his enemies and the fearful fate that awaited him, Daniel looked to his God.

For Daniel to have altered or terminated his prayer practice for the duration of the decree would have been cowardly defection. For him to have done so would have meant the condemnation of an accusing conscience, the certain loss of the approval of God upon him, and the bringing of moral disgrace upon himself in the eyes of his plotting opponents. Even Daniel's enemies did not expect him to do such a thing; ironically, they were actually counting on his sturdy moral character to provide them with an accusation to bring before the king.

It cost Daniel to remain openly loyal to God in that hour of fierce testing. The cost of unwavering loyalty is always high. But in the hour when the price is paid, the man of victorious prayer is made. The triumph in prayer over satanic opposition is born amid the stress and strain of spiritual testing. Daniel probably little realized at the time how much his loyalty and faithfulness meant to God, but the day came when the angelic messenger took him into the divine secrets (10:21; 11:2) and addressed him as a "man greatly beloved" (9:23; 10:11, 19).

The present is the hour of testing for the Church of Christ. God is waiting to see whether we too will maintain our supreme loyalty to Him in these days of satanic wickedness, whether His Word will be firmly adhered to and His exhortations to work with Him through prayer will be heeded, whether the work of world evangelization will be aggressively pressed and supported through faithful intercession, whether His own people will prove themselves steadfast and loyal even unto death.

III. *The Consequences of His Praying*

Praying like that of Daniel's is sure to produce mighty results. The book of Daniel is the inspired record of the far-reaching consequences of his praying.

1. *Personal deliverance.* Daniel experienced spectacular deliverances in connection with his prayer ministry. The remarkable

revelation made to Daniel recorded in chapter 2, cancelling the edict of Nebuchadnezzar that all the wise men of Babylon should be slain, came in response to the prayer concern "that Daniel and his fellows should not perish with the rest of the wise men of Babylon" (2:18).

The story of Daniel's deliverance from the mouth of lions (chap. 6) is one of the most thrilling stories in Scripture. Daniel's enemies had forced the unwilling King Darius to cast Daniel into the den of lions, but Daniel's loyalty to God made possible a mighty breakthrough of divine power on his behalf. The deliverance was so spectacular that the king issued a universal decree proclaiming it as an act of God (6:25-27).

2. *Divine revelations.* In chapter 2 we have the thrilling story of how God made known to Daniel the forgotten dream of Nebuchadnezzar in response to the united supplication of Daniel and his companions (2:18-19). God used this revelation of the king's dream and its interpretation to assure the personal safety of Daniel, to teach the haughty king a stirring lesson concerning His true nature (2:46-47), and to provide mankind with a vivid demonstration of His sovereign purposes with mankind in history, with a clear indication of the sure climax of the ages.

Chapters 9 through 12 record further revelations of profound importance which were explicitly given to Daniel in answer to his prayers. It is deeply impressive to note in how many ways the heavenly world assisted Daniel in his desires to know the deep things of God. When Daniel received a vision while at Shushan and sought to understand it, the angel Gabriel was sent to "make this man to understand the vision" (8:16). In chapter 9 Gabriel is again sent to give Daniel "skill and understanding" (9:22) in connection with the prophecy of the "seventy weeks" (9:24-27), one of the basic prophecies of Scripture. In 10:21 an angelic being announced to Daniel, "I will shew thee that which is noted in the scripture of truth." (Cf. also 11:2.) Daniel, the great man of prayer, was truly a God-taught man.

3. *Angelic activity.* Perhaps the most astonishing result of Daniel's praying is the revelation that it set the supernatural world into motion. In chapter 9 we see that as soon as Daniel began his Scripturally based prayer, activity commenced in heaven. Gabriel was at once caused to fly swiftly to give Daniel the needed spiritual understanding concerning God's messianic program

(9:21-22). As soon as God found a man who was moved and spiritually concerned about God's purposes, He began to work.

Even more dramatic is the revelation in chapter 10 of the supernatural repercussions of Daniel's prayer. The events in this chapter occurred some three years after those recorded in chapter 9. Apparently Daniel was perplexed and deeply burdened at the meager response to the royal decree permitting the return of the Jews to their own land (Ezra 1:1-4). Burdened in soul, he prayed for three weeks, determined not to give up until the answer came. At the end of that time he received his answer and was given an astonishing revelation concerning the cause of the delay. The angelic messenger informed Daniel that "the prince of the kingdom of Persia withstood me one and twenty days: but, lo, Michael, one of the chief princes, came to help me" (10:13). The angelic prince had started at once in response to Daniel's prayer, but he had been fiercely opposed by evil powers. Daniel's prayer had set off a gigantic spiritual conflict in the unseen realms. Billheimer concludes "Although the answer to his prayer was granted and already on the way, if Daniel had given up it presumably would never have arrived. Therefore the real battle was fought and the victory won in the place of prayer down on the river bank. The decisive action was there."[10]

This revelation to Daniel gives us a startling unfolding of the true scope and effect of vital prayer. The prayer of God's people causes definite action and conflict in "heavenly places." Prayer is thus seen to be a wrestling "against principalities, against powers, against the rulers of the darkness of this world, against spiritual wickedness in high places" (Eph. 6:12). These satanic forces are organized in their efforts to influence and control the governments of the world, and believers must break satanic powers through Spirit-empowered intercession. World conditions today reveal how strategically the Devil is deploying his forces in the conflict. May God raise up more intercessors among His saints who will actively enter into this struggle to thwart the forces of Satan!

Spirit-empowered, Bible-based praying is working with God at the very point where the action lies!

Notes

[1]Edward Dennett, *Daniel the Prophet: And the Times of the Gentiles* (1919; reprint ed., Denver: Wilson Foundation, 1967), p. 22.

[2]M. R. DeHaan, *Daniel the Prophet* (Grand Rapids: Zondervan, 1947), p. 186.

[3]Dennett, p. 137.

[4]W. C. Stevens, *The Book of Daniel* (1915; reprint ed., Los Angeles: Bible House of Los Angeles, 1943), pp. 131-32.

[5]Clarence Larkin, *The Book of Daniel* (1929; reprint ed., Philadelphia: Clarence Larkin Est., 1944), p. 24.

[6]O. Zöckler, "The Prophet Daniel," in *Lange's Commentary on the Holy Scriptures* (1870; reprint ed., Grand Rapids: Zondervan, n.d.), 13:60.

[7]Stevens, p. 24.

[8]Frederick A. Tatford, *The Climax of the Ages. Studies in the Prophecy of Daniel* (1953; reprint ed., London: Oliphants, 1964), p. 95.

[9]John Calvin, *Commentaries on the Book of the Prophet Daniel* (Reprint ed., Grand Rapids: Eerdmans, 1948), 1:359.

[10]Paul E. Billheimer, *Destined for the Throne* (Fort Washington, Pa.: Christian Literature Crusade, 1975), pp. 107-8.

Bibliography

1. Biblical Texts

American Standard Version. *The Holy Bible Containing the Old and New Testaments.* New York: Thomas Nelson & Sons, 1901.

English, E. Schuyler, et al., eds. *The New Scofield Reference Bible.* New York: Oxford University Press, 1967.

King James Version. *The Holy Bible Containing the Old and New Testaments.* Nashville: Holman Bible Publishers, 1979.

Montgomery, Helen Barrett. *The New Testament in Modern English.* Philadelphia: Judson Press, 1924.

New American Standard Bible. Carol Stream, Ill.: Creation House, 1971.

New English Bible. Oxford and Cambridge: University Press, 1970.

New International Version. *The Holy Bible Containing the Old Testament and the New Testament.* Grand Rapids: Zondervan, 1978.

Scofield, C. I., ed. *The Scofield Reference Bible.* New York: Oxford University Press, 1917.

Verkuyl, Gerrit, ed. *The Modern Language Bible, The New Berkeley Version.* Grand Rapids: Zondervan, 1969.

Weymouth, Richard Francis. *The New Testament in Modern Speech.* Revised by James Alexander Robertson. 5th ed. New York: Harper and Brothers, 1929.

Williams, Charles B. *The New Testament. A Private Translation in the Language of the People*. 1937. Reprint. Chicago: Moody Press, 1949.

Young, Robert. *The Holy Bible Consisting of the Old and New Covenants Translated According to the Letter and Idioms of the Original Languages*. London: Pickering & Inglis, n.d.

2. Books

Alexander, Joseph Addison. *Commentary on the Prophecies of Isaiah*. 1875. Reprint (2 vols. in 1). Grand Rapids: Zondervan, 1953.

Bernard, J. H. *The Pastoral Epistles*. Cambridge Greek Testament for Schools and Colleges. 1899. Reprint. Cambridge: University Press, 1922.

Billheimer, Paul E. *Destined for the Throne*. Fort Washington, Pa.: Christian Literature Crusade, 1975.

Broadus, John A. *Commentary on the Gospel of Matthew*. 1886. Reprint. Grand Rapids: Kregel, 1990.

Calvin, John. *Commentaries on the Book of the Prophet Daniel*. Translated by Thomas Myers. 2 vols. Reprint. Grand Rapids: Eerdmans, 1948.

Chadwick, G. A. "The Book of Exodus." In *An Exposition of the Bible*. Vol. 1. Hartford, Conn.: The S. S. Scranton Co., 1903.

Coates, C. A. *An Outline of the Book of Exodus*. Kingston-on-Thames, England: Stow Hill Bible and Tract Depot, n.d.

Curtis, Edward Lewis, and Albert Alonzo Madsen. *A Critical and Exegetical Commentary on the Books of Chronicles*. The International Critical Commentary. New York: Charles Scribner's Sons, 1910.

DeHaan, M. R. *Daniel the Prophet*. Grand Rapids: Zondervan, 1947.

Delitzsch, Franz. *Biblical Commentary on the Prophecies of Isaiah*. 2 vols. Translated by James Martin. Reprint. Grand Rapids: Eerdmans, 1949.

Dennett, Edward. *Daniel the Prophet: And the Times of the Gentiles*. 1919. Reprint. Denver: Wilson Foundation, 1967.

Eadie, John. *A Commentary on the Greek Text of the Epistle of Paul to the Colossians*. Edinburgh: T. & T. Clark, 1884.

Ellicott, Charles J. *A Critical and Grammatical Commentary on the Pastoral Epistles*. Andover, Mass.: Warren F. Draper, 1865.

Elmslie, W.A.L. "The First and Second Books of Chronicles." In *The Interpreter's Bible*. Vol. 3. New York: Abingdon, 1954.

Fairbairn, Patrick, ed. *Imperial Standard Bible Encyclopedia, Historical, Biographical, Geographical and Doctrinal*. 6 vols. 1891. Reprint. Grand Rapids: Zondervan, 1957.

Fausset, A. R. *Bible Cyclopaedia, Critical and Expository*. Hartford, Conn.: The S. S. Scranton Co., 1902.

Gaebelein, Arno C. *The Annotated Bible*. Reprint (9 vols. in 4). Chicago: Moody Press, 1970.

Goforth, Rosalind. *How I Know God Answers Prayer*. Grand Rapids: Zondervan, 1921.

Greenfield, John. *Power from on High*. Atlantic City, N.J.: The World Wide Revival Prayer Movement, 1931.

Guthrie, Donald. *The Pastoral Epistles*. The Tyndale New Testament Commentaries. Grand Rapids: Eerdmans, 1957.

Harvey, H. "Commentary on the Pastoral Epistles, First and Second Timothy and Titus; and the Epistle of Philemon." In *An American Commentary on the New Testament*. Vol. 6. 1890. Reprint. Philadelphia: The American Baptist Pub. Society, n.d.

Hendriksen, William. *Exposition of Colossians and Philemon*. New Testament Commentary. Grand Rapids: Baker, 1964.

————. *Exposition of the Pastoral Epistles*. New Testament Commentary. Grand Rapids: Baker, 1947.

Hervey, A. C. et al. "I Timothy." In *The Pulpit Commentary*. Vol. 21. Reprint. Chicago: Wilcox and Follett Co., n.d.

Jamieson, Robert, and A. R. Fausset. *A Commentary, Critical and Explanatory on the Old and New Testament*. Vol. 1. *Old Testament*. Hartford, Conn.: The S. S. Scranton Co., n.d.

Johnstone, P. J. *Operation World. A Handbook for World Intercession*. Bromley, Kent, England: STL Publications, 1978.

Keil, Carl Friedrich. *Biblical Commentary on the Prophecies of Ezekiel*. Translated by James Martin. 2 vols. Reprint. Grand Rapids: Ecrdmans, 1950.

————. *The Books of the Chronicles*. Biblical Commentary on the Old Testament. C. F. Keil and F. Delitzsch, eds. Translated by Andrew Harper. Reprint. Grand Rapids: Eerdmans, 1950.

Kuhn, Isobel. *Nests Above the Abyss*. Philadelphia: China Inland Mission, 1947.

Lange, John Peter. "Exodus." In *Lange's Commentary on the Holy Scripture, Critical, Doctrinal and Homiletical*. Vol. 2.

Exodus-Leviticus. 1876. Reprint. Grand Rapids: Zondervan, n.d.

Larkin, Clarence. *The Book of Daniel.* 1929. Reprint. Philadelphia: Rev. Clarence Larkin Est., 1944.

Lee, Harrington C. *St. Paul's Friends.* London: The Religious Tract Society, 1918.

Lenski, R.C.H. *The Interpretation of St. Mark's and Luke's Gospels.* Columbus, Ohio: Lutheran Book Concern, 1934.

————. *The Interpretation of St. Paul's Epistles to the Colossians, to the Thessalonians, to Timothy, to Titus and to Philemon.* Columbus, Ohio: Lutheran Book Concern, 1937.

Lightfoot, J. B. *Saint Paul's Epistles to the Colossians and to Philemon.* 1879. Reprint. London: Macmillan and Co., 1900.

Macbeth, John. *What Is His Name?* London: Marshall, Morgan & Scott, n.d.

McConkey, James H. *The Surrendered Life.* Pittsburgh: Silver Pub. Society, 1927.

Maclaren, Alexander. "The Epistles of St. Paul to the Colossians and Philemon." In *An Exposition of the Bible.* Vol. 6. Hartford, Conn.: The S. S. Scranton Co, 1903.

Martin, Ralph P. *Colossians: The Church's Lord and the Christian's Liberty.* Grand Rapids: Zondervan, 1972.

Martin, Roger. *R. A. Torrey, Apostle of Certainty.* Murfreesboro, Tenn.: Sword of the Lord Publishers, 1976.

Morgan, G. Campbell. *The Practice of Prayer.* New York: Revell, 1906.

Moule, H.C.G. *The Epistles of Paul the Apostle to the Colossians and to Philemon.* The Cambridge Bible for Schools and Colleges. 1893. Reprint. Cambridge: University Press, 1932.

Murray, Andrew. *With Christ in the School of Prayer.* New York: Grosset and Dunlap, n.d.

Nee, Watchman. *Let Us Pray.* New York: Christian Fellowship Publishers, 1977.

Plumptre, E. H., and T. Whitelaw. "The Book of the Prophet Ezekiel." In *The Pulpit Commentary.* Vol. 2. Reprint. Chicago: Wilcox and Follet Co., n.d.

Pollock, J. C. *Moody: A Biographical Portrait.* New York: The Macmillian Co., 1963.

Rawlinson, George. "The Book of Exodus." In *The Pulpit Commentary.* Vol. 2. Reprint. Chicago: Wilcox and Follett Co., n.d.

————. "The Second Book of Moses, Called Exodus." In *Ellicott's Commentary on the Whole Bible*. Vol. 1. Reprint. Grand Rapids: Zondervan, 1954.

Ryle, J. C. *Expository Thoughts on the Gospels*. Vol. 1. *Matthew–Mark*. Reprint. Grand Rapids: Zondervan, 1956.

Scott, E. F. *The Epistles of Paul to the Colossians, to Philemon and to the Ephesians*. The Moffatt New Testament Commentary. London: Hodder and Stoughton, 1936.

Stevens, W. C. *The Book of Daniel*. 1915. Reprint. Los Angeles: Bible House of Los Angeles, 1943.

Stevenson, Herbert F. *James Speaks for Today*. Westwood, N.J.: Revell, 1966.

Stull, Ruth. *Service on the Trail*. Philadelphia: Morning Cheer Book Store, 1944.

Tatford, Fredrick A. *The Climax of the Ages. Studies in the Prophecy of Daniel*. 1953. Reprint. London: Oliphants, 1964.

Tennyson, Alfred, Lord. *The Poetical Works of Alfred, Lord Tennyson*. London: Wark, Lock & Co., n.d.

Thomas, W. H. Griffith. *Christ Pre-Eminent. Studies in the Epistle to the Colossians*. Chicago: Moody Press, 1923.

Torrey, R. A. *How to Obtain Fullness of Power in Christian Life and Service*. 1897. Reprint. Wheaton, Ill.: Sword of the Lord Publishers, n.d.

Trench, Richard Chenevix. *Synonyms of the New Testament*. 1880. Reprint. Grand Rapids: Eerdmans, 1947.

Van Oosterzee, J. J. "The Pastoral Epistles." In *Lange's Commentary on the Holy Scriptures*. Vol. 22. *Thessalonians, Timothy, Titus, Philemon, Hebrews*. 1863. Reprint. Grand Rapids: Zondervan, n.d.

Vincent, Marvin R. *Word Studies in the New Testament*. Vol. 4. 1900. Reprint. Grand Rapids: Eerdmans, 1946.

Von Orelli, C. *The Prophecies of Isaiah*. Translated by J. S. Banks. Edinburgh: T. & T. Clark, 1895.

Ward, Ronald A. *Commentary on 1 & 2 Timothy & Titus*. Waco, Texas: Word Books, 1974.

White, Reginald E. O. *They Teach Us to Pray. A Biographical ABC of the Prayer Life*. New York: Harper & Brothers, 1957.

Zöckler, O. "The Prophet Daniel." In *Lange's Commentary on the Holy Scriptures*. Vol. 13. *Ezekiel–Daniel*. 1870. Reprint. Grand Rapids: Zondervan, n.d.

3. Periodicals

Cooper, David L. "The Prayer of Jabez." *Biblical Research Monthly* vol. 9, no. 1, (1944), pp. 3-4.

Dixon, A. C. "Prayer and Revival." *The Sword of the Lord*, 23 December 1949, pp. 1, 5.

"Prayer that is Good in God's Sight." *The Prophetic Word*, November 1949, pp. 614-17.

Indexes

Scripture Index

Subject Index

Jezebel, 15
Job, 93
John, 10, 14
Joshua, 47, 50, 52, 54-55, 63-64
Joshua, Seth, 86

Kuhn, Isobel, 15-16

Laodicea, 71, 78
Leavell, Roland Q., 12
Lone Star Mission, 86-87
Luther, Martin, 96

"Make me an Intercessor"
    (poem), 89
Mantel, J. Gregory, 41
Michael, 113
Moody, D. L., 21-22
Moravians, 30-31
"More things are wrought by
    prayer" (poem), 22-23
Morgan, G. Campbell, 22-23
Moses, 47-56, 94, 96
Mueller, George, 108

Nebuchadnezzar, 103, 105-6, 112
Nee, Watchman, 6, 31
Nehemiah, 15, 17
Nero, 40

"Oh, for a heart that is
    burdened" (poem), 36
"Oh, teach my will, my selfish
    will" (poem), 71-72
Onesimus, 70

Paul, 12-14, 16-17, 19, 35-44,
    69-78, 85, 96, 108
Peru, 20
Peter, 10, 14, 19, 20
Pharisees, 27
prayer
    example of Jabez, 59-66
    for laborers, 25-32
    intercession, 38
        call for, 28-32

empowerment through,
    47-56
example of Daniel, 101-13
example of Epaphras, 69-78
example of Moses, 47-56
God's demand for, 81-89,
    91-98
ministry of the Church, 35-45
nature of, 4-7
power of, 9-23
"prayers" (general term), 38
privilege of, 1-4
supplications, 1, 37-38
thanksgiving, 38, 105

Roberts, Evan, 86
Robinson, Forbes, 75

Sadducees, 14
Samuel, 50, 96
Sanballat, 17
Sanhedrin, 14
Satan (the Devil), 9, 49, 52, 55,
    93, 113
Saul, 50
Scott, P. Cameron, 30
Seekers After God, 92
Sennacherib, 15
Shephardson, Jennie E., 98
Solomon, 107
Stull, Ruth, 20-21

Taylor, J. Hudson, 13, 17
Tennyson, Alfred, Lord, 23
"There is a power that man can
    wield" (poem), 3-4
Theresa, St., 64
"There's a holy, high vocation"
    (poem), 45
"The world looks out of weary
    eyes" (poem), 98
Tobiah, 17
Torrey, R. A., 11, 52, 86
Tychicus, 73